Royce's
Voyage
Down
Under

Royce's Voyage Down Under

A Journey of the Mind

Frank M. Oppenheim

THE UNIVERSITY PRESS OF KENTUCKY

Library of Congress Cataloging in Publication Data
Oppenheim, Frank M   1925-
   Royce's voyage down under

   Includes bibliographical references and index.
   1. Royce, Josiah, 1855-1916. I. Title.
B945.R64066   191   79-4007
ISBN: 978-0-8131-5405-3

Scholarly publisher for the Commonwealth,
serving Berea College, Centre College of Kentucky,
Eastern Kentucky University, The Filson Club,
Georgetown College, Kentucky Historical Society,
Kentucky State University, Morehead State University,
Murray State University, Northern Kentucky University,
Transylvania University, University of Kentucky,
University of Louisville, and Western Kentucky University.

Editorial and Sales Offices: Lexington, Kentucky 40506

Contents

Preface

To restore his health, American philosopher Josiah Royce sailed around the world in mid-1888. He reported achieving significant philosophical growth while voyaging "down under" in the South Seas. To investigate this report, the present study tries to measure Royce's growth in metaphysics, ethics, and sociopolitical thought during his sojourn in Australasia. Thus the title, "Royce's Voyage Down Under," includes several levels of meaning: geographical, psychological, and philosophical. When Royce began his 1888 trip to Australia, he was "down under" psychologically. But soon he penetrated down under his previous depths of thought and gained a central insight that radiated into the broadest ranges of his thought. To set this insight of 1888 into the context the present study calls for, a survey of Royce's overall intellectual development may prove helpful.

Josiah Royce was born of pioneer parents in 1855 at Grass Valley, California. When, as a young boy, Josiah strolled amid the scenes of this mining town in the Sierra Nevada, he already was pondering the meaning of human history, life, and death.[1] Before graduating from the University of California at Berkeley in 1875, he had so steeped himself in contemporary British thinkers that he confessed of his undergraduate years, "I became through [John Stuart] Mill's influence a decidedly sceptical critical empiricist."[2] During the next seven years (1875-1882), though mentally still sloshing around in the swamp of sceptical empiricism, this youthful, largely self-made philosopher strove by his careful, persevering researches to reach a sound theory of knowledge.

His earnest pursuit of philosophy took him to Germany for a year of study under several outstanding professors and then to America's first graduate school for two more years of philosophical investigation at the Johns Hopkins University in Baltimore. For his doctoral dissertation Royce scrutinized precisely what we do when we make true judgments. Then serving as an instructor in English back at Berkeley from 1878 to 1882, Royce invested his private hours in insistently more critical investigations of the knowing self. He analyzed how in each present experience the self generates meaning by its unavoidable "postulates" of a past and a future. Answering a call to Harvard in the fall of 1882, Royce nurtured this invitation into a thirty-three-year career of teaching philosophy.

During his second semester at Harvard—in the spring of 1883—Royce finally broke through to his fundamental "religious insight."[3] This freed him from his "earlier sceptical position" and gave his mind that definitive orientation in which it persisted during all the subsequent transformations in the scope, manner, and spirit of his thought.[4] Shortly before his death in 1916, Royce looked back upon these early crises and declared that the years "1875 to 1883 determined my philosophical thinking."[5]

Because he estimated his religious insight as the basic light constituting his own philosophy, it seems necessary to distinguish between his "preformed" period (before 1883) and his "formed" period (after 1882). By this distinction I mean to indicate whether or not his "religious insight" was at work. Even as late as 1916, however, Royce's mind had not yet reached that wholeness of vision he had always sought.

But by then, a wiser Royce was much more modest, fallible, and ready to admit his limitations.

In brief, then, I view Royce's intellectual development as characterized chiefly by three maximal insights, which occurred in the pivotal years of 1883, 1896, and 1912.[6] These insights stimulated transformative reinterpretations of Royce's own thought and amounted to distinct additions to his former position. Yet the three resultant "changes of state" were at their vital central core sufficiently coherent to preserve the radical unity of his idealism. Thus in some first groping comparisons, one can liken the thought growth of Royce's "formed" period to the changes of state which an H_2O molecule undergoes when under heat it passes from ice, through water, to steam, or to the three growth stages of a butterfly which develops as a single self-identical, living reality from fertilized larva, through cocooned pupa, to adult four-winged organism.

Before each of these critical points of further penetration, Royce encountered a gradual cumulation of challenges, insights of minor or medium intensity, further criticisms, and increasing pressures. To each of these Royce responded through his commitment to seek more truth by breaking through in 1883 to the distinctively "new light" of the all-knowing Judge; in 1896, to the self-constituting, unavoidably social, Absolute Individual; and in 1912, to Reality as a Community of Interpretation, thanks to his realistic synthesis of hints drawn from the apostle Paul and the American logician, Charles Sanders Peirce. After each of these maximal insights, Royce's mind strove to reorganize his previous thought by reinterpreting all of it in terms of his latest "new growth." And the result each time was a synthesis, concreteness, tone, and expansion which were new.

On the basis of these three maximal insights, then, I differentiate his thirty-three years as a philosopher at Harvard into three subperiods: the early Harvard Royce (1883-1895), the middle Royce (1896-1911), and the mature Royce (1912-1916). Serious consequences flow from this way of dividing his thought growth but I believe the division is determined more by signals that Royce himself left about his philosophical pilgrimage than by my own doing.

More specifically, Royce's 1883 "religious insight" consisted in his finding enough evidence to abandon his former sceptical empiricism and its conseqent total ethical relativism. By fittingly and profoundly reflecting on his questions in theory of knowledge, in ethics, and in religion, he finally broke through to certain irreversible insights ("absolute truths") about the possibility of logical, ethical, and religious error. Coming to a peak in early 1883, these reflections opened upon an all-knowing Thought, discovered existentially present in the knowledge of error as error. Royce viewed his argument for this as "essentially altered" from that of his previous mode of thinking.[7] This breakthrough stemmed from what Royce called "the decided reversal" of his view about his postulates.[8] For these could not even be erroneous except within a community of knowers integrated by an All-Knower.

This intellectual penetration of 1883 needs to be seen within the matrix that helped form it. Royce's seven previous years of philosophical research into the theory of knowledge had accustomed him to "rather insistent self-criticism." Particularly during the last four years in his then philosophically barren California (1878-1882), he had sharpened his criticality by scrutinizing the basic structures of his consciousness. His Berkeley studies of "old Father Kant" had honed his understanding of the three *Critiques*, expecially Kant's notion of the kingdon of ends. Royce's intellectual reflections had already led him to experience intuitively that "beings with minds" cannot authentically intend the unending disharmony of all moral agents. Because every attempt to deny this intent to harmony simply reinstates it, Royce viewed this insight as irreversible and expressive of an invariant "internal meaning" in the self. At its innermost core this "internal meaning" constantly intends to promote, in and through every choice, a universal community of all moral agents.

With his move to Harvard in 1882, Royce's mental environment also changed. He found himself among intellectually more stimulating colleagues who did not automatically reject such thinking as "metaphysical daydreaming." Rather they challenged him to provide rational grounds for his theory. Moreover, some Harvard students asked him for guidance in their problems with life.[9] Upon discovering his moral and religious insights, Royce thought he could give such guidance. He grounded it on the community of human truth-seekers, cointended by a superhuman all-knowing Judge, its Norm. During the following decade (1883-1892), this idea of community guided Royce's works in history, the novel, and social psychology, as well as that highly organized philosophical idealism he expressed in the latter part of his *Spirit of Modern Philosophy* (1892). Royce's growth during his 1888 health cruise to Australia—the focus of the work at hand—occurred in the middle of this decade and resulted in a medium-range insight that injected new life and power into Royce's philosophizing.

By 1892, however, Royce's mind was already moving toward his second major penetration, his insight into what we mean by the individual. Already in 1891, a cue from logician Ernst Schroeder led Royce to see that whether one's metaphysical interpretation of the world be "realistic" (read "materialistic" and "agnostic") *or* "idealistic" (read "spirit-centered" and "theistic"), one's *ultimate meaning* of Reality could only be defined in terms of self-reflective individual elements which are serially, socially, and unendingly bound in unity.[10] Then from 1893 onwards, he was for several years strongly influenced by Francis H. Bradley's *Appearance and Reality*, as he later acknowledged.[11] But it was G. H. Howison who, perhaps even more than Schroeder or Bradley, jarred Royce into taking individuals seriously and into preserving human individuals from being absorbed by the Absolute. For during and after the famous 1895 "Conception of God" discussion at Berkeley, Howison fired enough shafts into Royce's at first loosely fastened armor that Royce was driven to search for a philosophically more adequate definition of the individual.[12] In his early-1896 Augustus Graham Lectures, Royce made what was, to my knowledge, the first public mention of his new penetration to the individual as "the object of exclusive interest." He arrived at this insight differently than he had done in 1883. For in the earlier year he had proceeded from a finite, erring, human self to an All-Knower. But in 1896 he argued from the freely self-constituting Absolute Individual to the finite imitations of this individualizing way of constituting a self.

Royce found this theory of individuality "unexpected" and "startlingly original."[13] Fortunately, several events then occurred which let Royce organize this "new light" and systematize his thought to the utmost. Challenged by the invitation to present the Gifford Lectures, Royce invested his consummate metaphysical energies in the writing of *The World and the Individual*. In the spring of 1898, he drank in C. S. Peirce's Cambridge Lectures entitled "Reasoning and the Logic of Things." Three years later, Royce in retrospect disclosed to William James, "[Those Peirce lectures] . . . will always remain epoch-marking for me. They started me on such new tracks."[14] Then late in 1899, having agreed to offer the Ingersoll Lecture on Immortality, Royce in it profoundly analyzed what we mean by an individual, using only the close of the lecture to draw out the implications for immortality. Royce's middle-period synthesis revealed not only Peirce's emphasis on logic and his "epoch-marking" ideas, but also Royce's own originality, which was shown, for example, in his view of the self as a "dynamo of ideas." Putting his insight of the serially self-constituting individual to work, Royce plowed into a direct examination of "life and life problems." Furthermore, in his 1901-1911 researches in logic, human truth, immortality, and illusions affecting race relations he almost explicitly formulated his latent awareness that the self has its teleological identity in the Beloved Community. In his *Philosophy of Loyalty* (1908), he did become explicitly aware of this and made it the heart and lifeblood of his ethics and metaphysics.

Coming to the third and final stage of Royce's thought growth, we sense that its expanse and wealth deserve a full-length study. Royce compared this "new growth" of 1912 to that kind of "unexpected" transformation in thought which he had experienced in 1883 when he passed from agnostic empiricism to theistic idealism.[15] We need not force this comparison by Royce into an admission that in 1912 his basic view was "essentially altered," as was the case in his 1883 breakthrough. But 1912 certainly marked a radical reinterpretation of his former ideas, a "distinct addition to my former position, a new attainment," as Royce appraised it.[16]

Although his 1912 apoplexy temporarily restrained his bodily movements, it seems only to have occasioned a new setting of directions for his mental energies. It did mean abandoning his dream of producing a masterwork in logic. However, Royce's temporary freedom from teaching allowed him to restudy C. S. Peirce's thought more carefully. He also reassessed the apostle Paul and Christianity as no other "classic" American philosopher had ever done. Little wonder, then, that this 1912-1916 period of his authentic maturity in thought is marked by the phrases "Community of Interpretation" and "life in the Spirit." These are clues of his deepened grasp of Peirce and Paul, working to appreciate more accurately the essence of the Christian creed, published in his mature masterpiece, *The Problem of Christianity* (1913).

Soon Royce carefully and explicitly described how he had recently and radically transformed his own theory of knowledge.[17] He had removed it from a subject-object basis and fitted it on the triadic relation of what he called technically a "Community of Interpretation." By doing this he found his philosophy becoming more concrete and meaningful. He also found it relating anew to inductive science's presuppositions and methods. What Royce had no need to mention here, since he had clearly stated it in his *Problem of Christianity*, was that this new concreteness, significance, and closeness to science came about through a new kind of immersion into the psychosocial order of time. This immersion avoided becoming a plunge into James's stream of *merely* casual continuities because, beyond mere tychism, Royce in his musing had detected that the teleology of a spiritual process unites finite minds and an inmost synchronological Interpreter in mutual presence and interaction.

In résumé, it seems oversimplified to depict Royce's overall thought growth merely as a straight-arrow emergence of the idea of the community. Rather, his intellectual development seems to show three ideas arising to explicit form, each in its own time and way. These were the ideas of community, individual, and Spirit, each intending its real counterpart at work within the world's universal Process of Interpretation. The idea of community (of human and superhuman cointenders and cointentions) was clearly present to Royce in the moral and religious insights of his early Harvard days. Yet through the subsequent decades his continuous social approach to philosophy lifted this idea to a new prominence.

Finally, his 1912 "breakthrough" to Peirce's distinctive philosophical method of interpretative musing brought the idea of community to center stage. The second central idea to emerge into explicit articulation was that of the individual. Surfacing definitively in 1896, it was later purified in many ways. This idea was socially defined, serially realized, and infinitely durational. The constructive work of Royce's middle period—especially as found in *The World and the Individual*—resembles a cocoon around this pupa of the individual. Finally, the idea of Spirit, often foreshadowed, began to show itself clearly when Royce studied loyalty.[18] Once Royce drew clues for his philosophy of religion from the vital ideas of Christianity, the presence of the idea of Spirit became pervasive. He presented the Spirit as a living bond of individual and the community, and as the Great Interpreter who mediates between participating members and their communities.

After this sketch of Royce's intellectual growth during more than four decades (1875-1916), the reader may wonder why in the present study we concentrate on merely a half year of Royce's life. Are not several competent overall surveys of his thought growth already available?[19] Are not full-length intellectual biographies of Royce in the making?[20] True enough. But the present investigation of Royce's intellectual development in 1888 is both timely and worthwhile because of at least four concurring facts.

First, only in his Australasian writings did Royce allow himself any major expression of his sociopolitical views. This fact alone makes his reflections on his 1888 experience particularly significant and deserving of study. Second, many interested in the history of American thought incline to the view that Royce became conscious of his loyalty doctrine only shortly before 1907 when he published his widely read *Philosophy of Loyalty*. But his Australasian writings show that Royce had already formed a rather well developed philosophy of loyalty almost two decades earlier. Third, the 1888 Royce discovered the significance of the appeal-and-response dynamism in community and founded his doctrine of loyalty on this transactional basis.[21] Most of all, however, if exception is made of Royce's logical interest, this Australian interlude manifests his *wholeness* in personality and in philosophy. Hence, an investigation of the 1888 Royce allows us to integrate the many facets of Royce the man and the thinker and to transcend a one-dimensional approach which so many studies have been compelled to take. These four facts, then, call for a concentrated investigation of Royce's intellectual growth during his brief visit to Australasia.

Ironically, Royce's 1888 insight into community arose precisely when he was removed from the highly intellectual and competitive communities of Harvard University, its philosophy department, and his own family, and was thrust first into solitude and then into nonacademic associations with his ship's captain and crew, with politicians and their parties, and with primitive Maoris and an Australian backwoodsman. Plunged into the vital interaction between elemental nature and his own organism, into the simple direct life of the crew, politicians, and primitives, and into the divine presence, Royce was rescued from his own abstractions and from Harvard's rarefied academic atmosphere.[22] Ironically, too, Royce's insight into loyalty as the vital center of community was occasioned by his lack of concern for his own health and thus by his disloyalty toward himself, his family, and his university. A third irony was that some of his readers branded him a disloyal American when his insight into loyalty led him frankly to expose the shortcomings of the widespread view that any genuine American is against the government, community organizations, and big institutions.

The theme unifying the present work is Royce's wholeness of multifaceted personality and of philosophically com-

plex-yet-simple mind. The central idea integrating his philosophical wholeness is community—that same idea of community which Royce in the final year of his life acknowledged
had risen only gradually to consciousness at the center of his
intellectual development.[23] Moved by the political and nonpolitical social experiences of his voyage of 1888, Royce
focused on the idea of loyalty as the heart of his idea of community. With the aid of his earlier "religious insight," he
grasped intellectually that the life of genuine loyalty is possible only if one possesses a vital bond with the universal
community and with its Infinite Alter Ego.[24] In Royce's
metaphysical insight of 1888, he recognized that within this
wholesome community any self's appreciative knowing of reality must be given primacy over the self's freedom and activity if the self is to attain integrated wholeness. Recognizing
further that it is self-contradictory and thus absurd for any finite knower as such, or any community of finite knowers as
such, to claim that its knowing is complete and genuine,
Royce asserted the actuality of the Infinite Self and All-
Knower as a necessary condition for any genuine finite knowing. In this way he developed his metaphysical insight into a
systematic wholeness.

This speculative system, though needed, was inadequate
for Royce, since human selves are also called to dedicated
service of their communities and causes. This loyal service requires wise practical attitudes, criteria for discerning priorities, and the guidance of sane maxims—all of which Royce
began to formulate in his 1888 philosophy of loyalty. Upon
this practical basis he constructed his only systematic interpretation of an integral sociopolitical philosophy. The link-
ages between Royce's metaphysical, ethical, and sociopolitical thought bound the doctrinal content just surveyed into a
whole system centered in the idea of community as enlivened
by the idea of loyalty.

But the wholeness of Royce's 1888 philosophy also includes his philosophical method. Earlier he had pledged himself to philosophize "earnestly, independently, and reverently."[25] In 1888 Royce mused in just this way over the materials he sought to interpret—something the reader will understand by a kind of mental symbiosis if he here accompanies Royce on his philosophical reflections while "down under." At that period Royce had not yet reflexively formulated his philosophical method into a methodology. (His 1912 insight into C. S. Peirce's way of reasoning would enable him to do so later.)[26] But by entering into Royce's efforts to straighten out "the big metaphysical tangle about continuity, freedom, and the world-formula, which, as you remember, I had aboard with me when I started," and by following Royce's moves to weave these strands into a coherent fabric, the reader will analyze and synthesize with Royce as he fashions the tapestry of his 1888 thought.[27] The reader may also perceive how Royce's integrated personality supported all these philosophical endeavors and collaborated with them—whether Royce functioned as a patient aboard ship, as a conversationalist, as a hiker in the Blue Mountains, as a political student, as a son and brother, or as a dedicated member of Harvard's philosophy department writing to his friend and colleague, William James.

Acknowledgements are here made to those who permitted me to publish from Royce's manuscripts: the heirs of the Josiah Royce family and Richard Hocking; and to the following institutions that have made the present study possible by publishing Royce's writings or preserving them for research: *Atlantic Monthly*; George Braziller; Clark University Press; Houghton Mifflin; Little, Brown; Macmillan; Scribners; and the University of Chicago Press; along with Bancroft Library of the University of California; Boston Public

Library; Harvard University Archives; Houghton, Robbins, and Widener Libraries of Harvard University; Johns Hopkins University Library; National Library of Australia; and Yale University Library.

In concluding this preface, I wish to thank every person who helped me with this work—most of all, Professor David J. Hassel, S.J., without whose encouragement, patience, and gentle but persistent prodding this book would never have been brought to birth. Of the many others who contributed to this study, I must mention Professors John Clendenning, John E. Smith, and Richard Robin because their support, critiques, and suggestions made this investigation possible. I am particularly indebted to my fellow Jesuits of Xavier University, especially Robert W. Schmidt and the late Thomas G. Savage, for their editorial assistance, and to Mrs. Eunice Staples for her outstanding secretarial skills. For the opinions expressed here, however, and for the imperfections still remaining, I must assume the responsibility.

1

Introduction

In the spring of 1888, William James wrote from Harvard to George Santayana studying in Berlin: "Royce (broken down at last) is on his way to Australia. But he'll be as stout as ever next year."[1] James's forecast was accurate. Early in 1888, Josiah Royce (1855-1916), American philosopher of community, was exhausted. His doctor advised him to sail leisurely and alone to Australia. Royce took the three-month cruise from Boston to Melbourne, then enjoyed the natural beauty of Australia and New Zealand for two more months, and finally returned by way of California to Harvard for the autumn term of 1888.[2]

On his voyage certain events occurred that advanced Royce's intellectual development significantly. To give balance to our study it should be stated at once that on his Australian trip Royce did not grow intellectually as much as he did through his transformative insights of 1883, 1896, and 1912.[3] For these latter three were respectively the seeds of *The Religious Aspect of Philosophy*, of his revised version of *The Conception of God*, and of *The Problem of Christianity*. Yet when Royce ended his 1888 trip, he knew that he brought back to Cambridge more than simply a body and mind refreshed by a long vacation at sea. He was convinced that during this trip he had "bagged new game" philosophically. Hence he was eager to share it.[4] Before landing in Australia, he had written William James: "In fine, I have largely straightened out the big metaphysical tangle about continuity, freedom, and the world-formula, which, as you remember, I had aboard with me when I started, and I am ready to amuse you with a metaphysical speculation of a very simple, but, as now seems to me, of a very expansive nature, which does more to make the dry bones of my "Universal Thought" live than any prophesying that I have heretofore had the fortune to do."[5] This tantalizing news made William James reply, "I shall 'admire' to hear your final solution of the antinomies, and am eager *deswegen* [on that account] for your return."[6] Precisely what had occurred in Royce's thought during his 1888 sojourn? This question focuses the central aim of the present study.

For his recuperation the doctor had prescribed simply that he live alone on a sailing ship.[7] Yet Royce regained his health, thanks not only to his solitary union with nature but also to his communion with people, aboard and ashore. Was it this blending of creative solitude and stimulating dialogue within his mind that "largely straightened out the big metaphysical tangle about continuity, freedom, and the world-formula"? The question suggests a twofold approach to Royce through his solitary reflections and through his social relations during this Australian cruise.

According to Milton R. Konvitz's description, Royce's mind was "trying to control a bursting complexity of thought."[8] Even before his voyage to Australia, during a dozen years he had already nourished his philosophy from roots that were affective and aesthetic, conative and creative, as well as logical and rational, although it was to this last mentioned pair that his published work had directed more attention. To understand Royce adequately, then, we first need to acquaint ourselves with the many different functions he fulfilled during his 1888 sojourn, functions that reflect his many-sided personality. Such a strategy will bring us in line with the standard Royce set for anyone aiming to grasp his philosophy: namely, an understanding of Royce's own "essential temperament" as the unique determinant of his philosophizing.[9]

Even if we lack that "whole of the longer story" he wrote to his wife about his South Sea experience, what do the available letters from the trip and his written reflections on it suggest concerning his personality and temperament?[10] As a correspondent, Royce is frank, humorous, and noticeably self-revealing. As a patient, he is keenly alert to the "turns of weather" that his psyche undergoes during his convalescence. As a sensitive perceiver both of nature and of his own affective responses to it, he reveals how major changes of one's natural setting induce altered states of consciousness. As a fellow companion or hiker, he shows himself to be an artist of dialogue, a man of many lively interests, and a guest who is humanly flexible. Moreover, he is an insightful student of men and of their political systems. Along such general lines, we can in the first part of this study gain a closer acquaintance with the affective and volitional sides of his personality.

Under this set of sails, we can launch out next to fathom directly the intellectual depths he reached on his 1888 voyage. Our questions will then become: 1) In his solitary reflection, what discovery caused his new "metaphysical speculation"? 2) What deeper moral insight helped him better understand his ethical "question about Freedom and the Ideals"? 3) How did his new social relations stimulate a social and political philosophy given little expression until then?

What method guides our investigation in this second part of the study? Through textual analysis we assemble the available clues that Royce left of his intellectual growth in 1888, while keeping his first sketch and his marginalia on Martineau in subordinate positions. Then in the final part of the study we test our reading of these clues against a later, key, Roycean insight, against two of his leading philosophical works produced shortly after his return, and against the total context of his life's intellectual development.

In contradiction of our present aim and method, some objections readily arise. For example, it might be said that insights do not usually occur on health cruises. And if the marginalia on Martineau do stem from Royce's depressed period, it might be argued that they may not be used even as subordinate evidence. In briefest response here, it can be said that great minds often make key discoveries when relaxed after toil.[11] Secondly, intrinsic and extrinsic evidence suggests a postdepression dating of Royce's marginalia on Martineau, thus freeing them for a critical subordinate function in our study.

2

Context:
Voyage
and
Recuperation

Since his 1882 start at Harvard, Royce had passionately desired to succeed there. Psychologically his 1888 breakdown stemmed from his drive to become an accepted philosophical colleague within a prestigious department and from his ambition to win a full professorship eventually. In the beginning, he had to invest three years of demanding teaching to steady his first perilous perch in the department. Then, in addition to carrying out as an assistant professor of philosophy his full instructional duties of teaching fifteen to eighteen hours weekly at Harvard and at the Society for the Collegiate Instruction for Women (the future Radcliffe), he simultaneously saw through publication his first major philosophical work, his first volume in history and character study, and his first novel.[1] These protracted pressures took their toll. Royce was stout, but not superhuman. He doggedly pushed himself into the first semester of 1887-1888, and completed it. But on February 9, 1888, he confided to Daniel Coit Gilman, the guide of his intellectual life: "The breakdown is nervous of course and needs nothing, I am assured, but a long sea voyage all alone, to make me myself again. . . . I feel nearly all the time very well and nobody meeting me on the street would call me ill, but the little devil in the brain is there all the same, and this kind goeth not out but by travelings and hard fare."[2] That spring, the Harvard Corporation granted Royce a leave of absence at half pay. He indicated to Gilman that a "very dear friend" was financing the trip and insuring the safety and comfort of his family during his absence. Signs point to the ever-faithful Charles Rockwell Lanman as this friend, who also gifted Royce with smoking pipes, a three-month supply of tobacco, and a set of informative ocean charts.[3]

Others helped, too. George Herbert Palmer influenced President Eliot of Harvard to secure the services of that independent philosopher Francis Ellingwood Abbot. The latter would carry on Royce's advanced course in the philosophy of nature but in his distinctively non-Roycean way.[4] William James thoughtfully provided mineral water, figs, and some French novels. Serving as Josiah's secretary, his wife Katharine penned needed letters, assisted with the packing, and helped gather reading materials for the trip. Besides the French novels these included Cassanova's memoirs, some books in mathematics and mechanics, and, yes, those gift volumes of *A Study of Religion* just received from James Martineau in England.[5] Royce had an Australian acquaintance, Richard Hodgson, secretary of the American Society for Psychical Research, who provided him with introductions to friends in Australia.[6] Someone arranged passage with Captain Howes of the *Freeman*. And soon all was ready.

After two days of delay, the square-rigged *Freeman* finally weighed anchor from Boston on February 27. Lanman recorded that an awful storm tore at the sails of this bark as it faded out of sight and beyond Boston light into the wintry

North Atlantic trying to reach the more peaceful sum-
mertime of the southern seas. Just as perilously perched as
the *Freeman* was its invalid passenger, since Royce was
undergoing the crucial test whether his psyche could actually
survive its run-down condition and regain its full vigor. His
trial lasted longer than that of his ship. For soon it encountered twelve weeks of fair weather so that it sailed
leisurely into the South Atlantic, down to the Cape of Good
Hope, and then straight through the Indian Ocean towards
Melbourne, the capital of Victoria. Meanwhile Royce was
undergoing what he had expected: "a long siege of dull
spirits at the outset of the voyage."[7] Despite his "head-
weariness" at the start of the voyage, Royce's wits would whir
on mechanically. But his emotions were dull and motionless,
due to his "overtaxed nerves . . . uncomplicated by any
organic or other deep trouble." Fortunately, Royce was his
own best analyst and knew that his long period of depression,
if wisely handled, would be turned into part of an "experience . . . in many ways highly educating."[8] To William
James he described his flattened state as not strong enough to
be called "misery," even as he told of his cure:

It was an absolute negation of all active predicates of the emotional
sort save a certain (not exactly "fearful") looking-for of judgment
and fiery indignation. —But all this pathology is no longer in
order. With the winds and the birds of the southern sea came a new
life. . . . And now that passion has come again, and the good Lord
seems to have some life in his world of "*Sonnen und Milchstrassen*," my wits grow more constructive, and I more and more
look upon the voyage as a very highly educating experience.[9]

After nearly three months of sailing, Royce found "the sea a
perfectly satisfactory cure" for himself. Writing from off
Melbourne, he was "full of enthusiasm" and longed to go
hiking on dry land.[10]

Royce's interaction with nature dated from his child-hood. He had viewed the vistas of the Sacramento Valley, gazed meditatively at the Golden Gate, and hiked alone along pine trails on the Coastal Range. During his first six years at Harvard, when he added long journeys of laborious research and the pressures of publishing to his heavy academic load, such tastings of nature, while providing welcome relief, were very brief.[11] Now, however, during the first twelve uninterrupted weeks of his voyage, except for his routine contacts with the crew, Royce was immersed in nothing but nature. Its forces, working down upon him from the outside universe and up from within his own organism, wrought their cure physically and psychologically.

Royce's letters written "out of Melbourne" portray a person filled with a new zest for life. He believed in nature's tendency to initiate and integrate self-healing processes.[12] Moreover, as his regular hiking and regimen showed, he usually exercised some self-discipline to remain healthy. Not only did he write, "I am enjoying myself like a seabird," but also, "I am holding myself back from any hard work."[13] As the *Freeman* drew near Melbourne, by day and night Royce experienced nature's beauties afresh.[14] He began to sense a seemingly divine presence alive in all the "suns and milky ways" of the universe. All around him, in sea, sky, stars, and birds, he felt life passionately and, even more responsively, found himself appreciating the ship's captain and crew.

One vivid interaction occurred shortly after his landing in Australia, when Royce went hiking in the Blue Mountains. His account of this experience focused primarily on the human self's responses rather than on the mountains, valley, and waterfall which unleashed his moods and feelings.[15]

On this morning, in company with Alfred Deakin, later to become Australia's prime minister, Royce began hiking from his hotel high in the Blue Mountains. The two started in a "fairly level and well wooded region with pleasant streams visible here and there." Like many other visitors, however, Royce soon found the face of nature turning weird as the landscape became harsh and gaunt. The Royce who in his philosophy strove to include a "genuine romanticism" now wove into his account at least as many of his own feelings as facts about nature: "Suddenly your path becomes steep, rocky, lonesome. You seem to have left all signs of life far behind. The slopes, as you glance downward, look treacherous; and you wonder if they do not lead to the edge of some near abyss. And then, at a turn in the way, you come indeed to the abyss itself. The ground flies away from under your feet. A valley stretches out for many miles, and far beneath you. A sheer precipice of a thousand or fifteen hundred feet is directly below where you stand."[16] Here terms like "suddenly," "lonesome," "you glance downward," "treacherous," "you wonder if," and "ground flies away from under your feet," reflect how Wentworth Valley triggered a gamut of feelings in Royce. His "stream of consciousness" manner shows him more in touch with his own affections, memories, and fancies than with the valley.

Soon the sight of Wentworth Falls led him to draft an even deeper phenomenological description of what occurred within himself. Adopting the indefinite "one" and "you," he asserted that a majestic natural scene raises people's alertness, lures them fascinatingly, pacifies, and eventually tames them. This dialogue between the observer and nature as "other" is almost explicit in the following Roycean description of Wentworth Falls and the surrounding cliffs: "All this one sees standing himself at the edge of the abyss, the thrill of the scene quivering all through his nerves, the fascinating depths begging him to step from the rocks and try to imitate the water flight himself. . . . Such scenery, I have observed, usually first acts to make one very gentle and submissive in mood. One feels like a child watching a great multitude of busy folk. It is delightful, but it is also physically overwhelming. What is going on here is too large to be made out. It tames you. . . ."[17] Here Royce described how such scenery mysteriously alters our state of consciousness. While we are more or less attuned to nature's influences, yet we cannot rationally contain all the changes of feeling that occur in such an experience. Royce later noted how the gradually acquired attitudes and frameworks of adult nature-observers can often block out the simple brute freshness that a child experiences at Wentworth Falls and its surrounding cliffs.[18]

In starting philosophy, one is guided, said Royce, by one's temperament. And temperament is partly determined by one's feelings and moods towards nature. No need for this to degenerate into a sentimental romanticism, or *Schwarmerei*. An authentic employment of affectivity, a genuine romanticism, can be achieved through critical "in-touch-ness" with self and nature.[19]

Royce further recorded that in the Blue Mountains he felt a certain estrangement. This contrasted with his feelings of at-home-ness experienced when hiking in his native Sierra Nevada mountains. That he perceived the Blue Mountains as melancholy and solemn might have been due in part to this feeling of strangeness and aloneness. The valley's gnarled trees became for him symbols of evolutionary struggle. Its precipices struck fear into him and nature's unexpected turns evoked from him a feeling of treachery. Here Royce exemplified that rich mix of spontaneous affective movements whose lures, aversions, hopes, and fears provide the matrix of fruitful suggestions and captivating biases out of which rational philosophy must critically construct itself.[20] With William James and other thinkers, Royce fittingly acknowledged the inescapable dependence of philosophers and philosophy on a genuinely affective, even romantic, element.

We find that his heart skipped not only at beholding Wentworth Falls but also at sighting the volcanic regions of the North Island of New Zealand.[21] Several months later he recalled how sublime such scenes were when he again gazed at the woods and ridges of his beloved California. A similar experience occurred when he sped by Mount Shasta and later glimpsed the glory of the Canadian Rockies. Little wonder, then, that some of his writings of the 1888 period suggest Keats's theme, "Beauty is truth, truth beauty."

With Thomas B. Howes, captain of the *Freeman*, Royce shared some of his communing with nature.[22] While sailing through the tropic night, these two would sit on deck, gaze into the heavens, and talk over Newcomb's astronomy. With such stellar distances confronting them, they grew meditative, wondering whether stars and men were as unreal as dreams: Royce's delightful response has been published more than once.[23] But his humorous tale (which contrasts Mark Twain's very funny lectures with Joseph Cook's far less funny accounts) and his crude concluding parallel between "not so *damned* funny" and "not so *damned* real" often entertain readers so much that a key philosophical message is missed. For Royce's final remark was, "Even so, Captain, I teach at Harvard that the world and the heavens and the stars are all *real*, but not so *damned* real, you see."

Here the epistemologist pointed to more than our awareness of two levels of the real when we reflectively judge whether nature is real. For by indicating that in such self-possessed judgments the human self grasps its own knowing as more "damned real" than the stars, Royce added that our judgments of reality are also judgments of appreciation. This germinal idea that we grasp reality and value together flowered into explicit statement twenty-eight years later. In his last lecture on metaphysics, Royce taught, "The very recognition of being is itself an estimate."[24] Already in 1888, however, the contrast effect between himself and the natural world as an "other" had led him both to affirm two levels of reality and to prize selves more at the level of their unique affective subjectivity than at the level of their common abstract objectivity. This was a step towards his soon-to-be-published central distinction between the "World of Appreciation" and the "World of Description."[25]

Our two close-ups of Royce interacting with nature—with Deakin in Wentworth Valley, and with Captain Howes under the stars—show that nature touched Royce's affective and appreciative, as well as cognitive, potentials. William James noticed the same influence, even though he had only letters from the South Seas to go by. He exclaimed, "What a sight of the world you are getting, and how your cosmic emotions and your *empirisches Bewusstsein* must increase!"[26] Royce found nature quite rich, even mysterious, in her messages to us and saw dialogue with her as fundamental to any cosmology. It should not surprise us, then, that a few years later (1895), he clearly expressed these themes in his philosophy of nature: "Here about us, as we all admit, whatever our ultimate metaphysical views, is the natural world, the world that appears to our senses—a world manifesting some sort of finite, and obviously, as we mortals see it, some sort of highly fragmentary truth. . . . Our relations with nature are thus such as to involve a more or less social contrast between our life and the life of nature. And upon this principle every philosophy of nature must rest."[27] Here Royce viewed nature as alive and partially self-manifestative.[28] Basically, as alive and evolving, nature calls on our wills to appreciate its life, to experience its communication, and to reverence its luring mystery. This Roycean principle of interpretation, when animated by his commitment to engage "reverently . . . face to face with a mighty and lovely Nature," furnishes an incipient "ethics of ecology."[29]

Besides his healing contacts with nature, Royce found a tonic in the persons he met. He found the ship's company "a jolly one, on the whole," and "highly agreeable."[30] His contact with Captain Howes, a person untouched by the academic world, helped restore a new philosophical awareness in Royce. His interactions with James Martineau—later to be evaluated—stimulated his philosophical quest. With his new discoveries Royce became positively enthusiastic. He strongly felt the will to live so that he could share his new vision with William James and others. He "wanted nothing so much as to get back to work," and had to restrain this will to work.[31]

Once ashore in Australia, he found "very good companionship," partly thanks to Hodgson's helpful introductions. The chief secretary of Victoria was Alfred Deakin, and in early June of 1888, Royce and Deakin "found each other."[32] During hikes and conversations, such as the one in Wentworth Valley, each of them became in turn the other's pupil or teacher as the topic became philosophy or politics or some other forte of one of them. Royce found that Deakin embodied the best elements of Australia, and that he offered indeed the health-giving support Royce then needed.[33] Soon afterwards he wrote to Deakin, "I had been needing for some time a kind of championship that you gave me in an undeserved degree of fullness. I can't tell you how much you brightened me up."[34] Through the succeeding decades, despite the distance between them, these two men continued to cultivate by mail the special friendship they began in June 1888.

When in Sydney, thanks to Deakin's reports and newspaper accounts, Royce kept in touch with the Conference of the Society for the Federation (of the Australian states). He found its delegates highly interesting. Their factional choices of attitudes and policies intrigued him, as did the foreseeable effects of these choices upon themselves and "Australia."

For, at that time, their six self-governing colonies were quite independent of one another and would require thirteen more years to form a federation.

Then leaving Sydney in the company of another Australian political figure, Sir Saul Samuel, he headed for Auckland on the *Zealandia* and learned from Sir Saul a political viewpoint noticeably divergent from Deakin's.[35] He found New Zealand's climate and scenery an even more healthy balm than Australia's. In the land of the Maoris, he learned their ancestral story—how their tribe came from Hawaiki across risky ocean stretches to New Zealand, some even coming "in the canoe Tai-Nui."[36] These Maoris fascinated Royce for decades, not least of all because of their communal felt need to pass on from generation to generation the "ideal past event" of their original adventuresome coming to New Zealand.[37]

On the steamer *Alameda*, headed for San Francisco, Royce met a man from the backwoods of Australia. So much had this pioneer's rugged life schooled him into a masterful blend of self-reliance and complete dedication to his neighbors "in the bush" that Royce found in him—as we shall soon discover in more detail—the concretized idea of the "loyal man." Loyalty was again stressed in Royce's travels when he reached his family in California and found them distraught by the recent loss of his father. From his family he learned to appreciate even more the loyal responsibility of caring for his health lest he abandon those who depended on him.

During the latter half of his journey, then, Royce was reaching out, in respectful dialogue, to persons as different as Captain Howes, Deakin, Sir Saul, and the backwoodsman from Australia. He wholeheartedly and easily enjoyed most of them. Under their influence he took decisive initiatives impossible several months earlier when he was an apathetic patient. Now a lively will welled up through his personality. For instance, after reappraising his chances for a sounder cure in New Zealand, and after seeking counsel from Sir Saul, Royce had unexpectedly decided to remain there rather than to proceed as planned to the Sandwich Islands.[38] Moreover, looking back to the nadir just passed, Royce had reported, "I have found my will all sound."[39] And, as if in confirmation of this, he resolved to take greater care of his health in the future. Even more significant was his resolve, "But I won't let myself be discouraged." In these ways, then, the volitional side of Royce's temperament was reenlivened both by personal efforts and by his friends' support.

3

Metaphysical
Speculation

Acquaintance with Royce's temperament readies us to investigate his intellectual progress on his 1888 trip. Presumably the lengthy, journallike manuscript which Royce mailed from Australia to his wife would reveal something of his intellectual speculations aboard, for he acknowledged that only to her "have I tried to be anywhere nearly complete."[1] Yet even if extant, this document is not available in any archive known to Roycean scholars. Hence the crucial question becomes, How extensive, clear, and reliable are the main clues that are available to us?[2] Arranged chronologically, these are: Royce's first sketch with note (April 5 and 6), his marginalia on Martineau (about May 6), and the long letter Royce drafted to William James on May 21 while off Melbourne. An initial survey of these three pieces of evidence seems in order.

Royce's philosophical journal of 1888 begins with the heading "Barque Freeman, April 5, '88."[3] Without so much as a word to hint at his recent weeks of depression, Royce here articulated his new insight into an outline of a book to be called "The World as Paradox and as Ideal."[4] For him it was "the first sketch of a discussion of critical and constructive philosophy as now projected in the form of an essay." By April 5, then, Royce was clearly well enough to attempt some profound philosophizing. Otherwise, he could not have elaborated this plan for a systematic metaphysical work whose three books integrated seventeen chapters. Since he often recast this sketch once he had returned to Cambridge, he evidently viewed it as a tentative effort to express his new metaphysical speculation.[5]

Royce intended to begin his work by setting forth and illustrating "the fundamental issue between the necessity and freedom aspects of reality." This first sketch clearly reveals Royce already striving to straighten out the paradoxes arising from continuity, freedom, and the world-formula. He sought to clarify his insight by employing the analogy of differential coefficients and the mathematical logic they imply. In this draft he did not yet apply his speculation to loyalty or sociopolitical theory. He described his Universal Thought as an "Absolute Will [which] must know itself *as an infinity of arrested volitions.* . . . Each [of the latter] must be a concrete expression of the one universal tendency or inner law."[6] He echoed the concerns and spirit of Schopenhauer and Kant throughout this outline, and although he alluded to Wundt, Spencer, Spinoza, and the Stoics, nowhere did he yet mention James Martineau. However, Royce's handwriting slackened and showed fatigue as it neared the end of these sixteen pages of metaphysics. Meanwhile, his style of developing the chapter outlines into full paragraphs tapered off into simply jotting down bare or almost bare chapter headings.

Chronologically, our second main set of clues comes from the marginalia which Royce, during his Australian voyage, inscribed on his copies of James Martineau's *A Study of Religion.*[7] Finally, we possess Royce's letter of May 21, 1888, to

William James. Because of the limitations of letter writing, Royce despaired of describing adequately this "new specimen" even to his philosopher friend; yet we will find in this letter our critical source of evidence because of its disciplined faithfulness to Royce's recent intellectual experience.

To evaluate these three main sets of clues, we must use skill to avoid the extreme either of pressing them too hard or of failing to get fully in touch with them. Royce's original manuscript of "The World as Paradox and as Ideal" seems valid only as a subsidiary witness. When drafting this outline, he had not yet fully recovered his health. He later repeatedly recast it. Hence, we will not rely on this first sketch in the following critical analysis, except insofar as this earliest witness confirms our main findings through its tentative first signals of his new speculation.

Royce's marginalia on Martineau constitute a different kind of witness. They are critical philosophical responses rather than an attempt at system-building. Moreover, the final three-quarters of Martineau's *A Study of Religion* received Royce's penciled observations about a month after Royce first outlined his projected book—that is, when he certainly had grown in strength of body and vigor of mind. Therefore, while insisting on their subordinate rank, we will search these marginalia to discover what light, if any, they cast upon Royce's remarks to James about a new and enlivening metaphysical speculation.

First and foremost, however, we will rank Royce's May 21 letter to James. It is granted that the description of Royce's new insight is jejune and general. Nevertheless, this letter deserves to become our controlling text because it is disciplined internally by one philosopher's endeavor to communicate his revised metaphysics to a friendly but critical colleague.

Before we attempt to analyze Royce's May 21 letter to

James, let us read carefully in its wholeness the "confession" it contains. Royce sets the scene in his first two sentences; then beginning with "In fine," he describes his mind substantially.

With the winds and the birds of the southern sea came a new life. . . . And now that passion has come again, and the good Lord seems to have some life in his world of "*Sonnen und Milchstrassen*," my wits grow more constructive, and I more and more look upon the voyage as a very highly educating experience. In fine, I have largely straightened out the big metaphysical tangle about continuity, freedom, and the world-formula, which, as you remember, I had aboard with me when I started, and I am ready to amuse you with a metaphysical speculation of a very simple, but, as now seems to me, of a very expansive nature, which does more to make the dry bones of my "Universal Thought" live than any prophesying I have heretofore had the fortune to do. The fields of speculation are very wide and romantic, after all, and great is the fun of bringing down new game. I must live to tell about this new specimen, at any rate. But I despair of describing it to you in this letter. I must wait until we meet. Suffice it that the old trouble about Continuity has come to seem to me very enlightening for the whole range of metaphysics, but particularly for our question about Freedom and the Ideals. I can't imagine why people will thrash the old straw in discussing this question. Dear good Martineau runs the same old treadmill for half his book. The thing has endlessly numerous novelties in it, just because it is a burning problem of life. Why not be somewhat vital and personal in thinking out what is after all an immediate vital issue of every moment?—But alas! perhaps my suggestions will seem to you as arid and old as any others. But wait till we meet, and we shall see.[8]

Here Royce confessed finding a "metaphysical speculation" that gave new life to his earlier philosophy. According to the nexus suggested by his "In fine," the roots of his new speculation lay in his affective awakening, his freshened sense of a life-giving divine milieu in the universe, and his present "more constructive" trend of mind. The scope of his new speculation reached to cosmology, morals, and metaphysics—for he had largely unraveled the "tangle about continuity, freedom, and the world-formula." This interpretation of scope is confirmed by his use of "metaphysics" three paragraphs later in a portion of the letter not quoted above. There "metaphysics" means not only the relation of stars and the physical world to the world of the knowing, valuing, finite selves but also the relation of all these to the Cognitively Inclusive, Appreciating, Infinite Self.

For about five years Royce had viewed this basic, familiar, complex relation mainly along logical and epistemological avenues.[9] But now he wanted to be "vital" and "personal" in "thinking out . . . an immediate vital issue of every moment," in which this relation was immediately felt as "a burning problem of life." Fortunately, his "*Sonnen und Milchstrassen*" allusion to the conclusion of book 4 of Schopenhauer's *The World as Will and Presentation* unintentionally establishes a benchmark which locates and dates one significant outcropping of this life interest that was gradually becoming more dominant in Royce's thought. For he later revealed that after *The Religious Aspect*, rather than focusing mainly on the World as Presentation (as Object or Thought), he had found the World as Will and Experience (as Purpose and Appreciation of Value) growing more central in his interests.[10] Fittingly enough, a recently recuperated Royce perceived his basic metaphysical relation to be permeated now with life-giving and healing energies.

By balancing its contrasting marks, he described his "new speculation." It was "very simple" yet "very expansive." It was "an immediate vital issue of every moment," yet involved "very wide and romantic" fields of speculation. If Royce were not a "complex mind," such utterances might at first puzzle us. Yet he provided the nexus between the apparent contraries. "The thing has endlessly numerous novelties in it, *just because* it is a burning problem of life" (emphasis added). His insight into every moment's "vital issue" ceaselessly opened up new directions for exploring metaphysics, morals, and cosmology. Royce found great fun in "bringing down new game" like this, particularly since his struggle to understand continuity now led to new insights into freedom and the ideals. In sum, his burning life-problem seems to have been, How could the inmost self, not bound by continuity, yet confronted by the call of each moment's "whither now?" generate ideals and how could this self freely strive to embody these ideals by true willing rather than by blind willing?

His "Suffice it" revealed more specific clues. For Royce, the dark "old trouble about Continuity" has been transformed into a great light for all metaphysics.[11] This was especially true for his and James's "question about Freedom and the Ideals." Here Roycean readers discern a characteristic theme. Just as Royce had penetrated doubt to find certitude, and the possibility of error to find an Unerring Knower, so now had he not penetrated his old trouble about continuity to find at the heart of the trouble a noncontinuous, enlightening, free self? In brief, is he not moving here through his World of Description only to find that it requires a World of Appreciation from which it derives?[12]

To further illuminate the hints in this letter about his new "metaphysical speculation," we now turn to Royce's 1888 marginalia on Martineau. They reveal Royce's "complex mind," that is, they show how intricate was the "tangle about continuity, freedom, and the world-formula" with which he struggled.

As Royce sailed into the southern seas, he began to read

Martineau's two-volume *A Study of Religion*. He made only a few jottings in the first volume until Martineau had completed his evaluation of Royce's own *Religious Aspect of Philosophy*.[13] After that, the marginalia became more frequent and continued through the second volume.

Royce seems to have venerated Martineau much as he did his Harvard colleague, George Herbert Palmer—although he found both too pious to be rigorously logical. Martineau seemed "so warmhearted and sympathetic," even though too simple and unrealistic about the problem of evil.[14] In *A Study of Religion*, Royce was impressed by Martineau's refusal to go along with Comte or Spencer when they defined religion without God. Martineau had written: " . . .by Religion I understand the belief and worship of Supreme Mind and Will, directing the Universe and holding moral relations with human life."[15] After reading lines such as these, Royce interestingly altered what he then came to view as "the dry bones of my 'Universal Thought' " into an enlivening concrete Personal Self in communion with all finite selves. But it was a Self whose living Logos still retained priority over its free agency and power.[16]

Despite this insight, "dear good Martineau" irritated Royce on several counts. We find the penciled note: "But M. [Martineau] cares not whether he be mystical and romantic, or intellectual and prosaic. It is all one [to him]."[17] Such confusion of the mystical and logical modes of thought raised Royce's caution. Secondly, Royce felt that Martineau "declines to face fully and fairly . . . the difficulty that, in a moral world, a free agent should be permitted to cause another not merely to suffer, but to sin, to be morally degraded." Repeatedly Royce indicated that Martineau left "no room for the devil" and in general declined to face the problem of evil.[18]

Concerning his own *Religious Aspect of Philosophy*,

what critique did Royce receive from Martineau?[19] It was an "original and vigorous" work, said Martineau, who also acknowledged Royce's "brilliant ingenuity." But Martineau had serious reservations about Royce's Infinite Knower, who was "all-seeing, all-judging, right-thinking, but doing nothing and preventing nothing; it is the infinitude of Reason and the negation of will."[20] This critique found its mark, for Royce not only now began in earnest to jot dozens of notes in the margins of his copy of Martineau, but soon described the center of his previous philosophy as "dry bones." Some of Royce's marginalia ran to a page or more. From all of them, I select about a half dozen sets that seem most to illuminate his May 21, 1888, letter to James. But before entering into any discussion of these marginalia, we should perhaps note the method employed to interpret them.

Our order of considering these marginalia will generally be Royce's own order of writing them, supposing he read Martineau continuously. From the series of marginalia, the overall movement of Royce's thought emerges as follows. Royce moves from continuity through finite willing to Infinite Alter Ego, whose all-knowing is both the life-function that is more primordial than free agency or power (contrary to Martineau's view) and also the "true solution" of the problem of permitting moral evil.[21] Accordingly, the underlying metaphysical questions with which Royce seems serially to have grappled are: 1) Shall my primary route to metaphysics lie through the humanly experienced object or through the experiencing subject? 2) If the latter, shall my order in metaphysics move from agency and power to knowing as derivative (as in Martineau's order)? Or, rather, should my order move through power and agency down to infinite-knowing first as originative of true willing, then as permissively inclusive of false willing, and finally as constitutive of Being? Royce opted for the latter order. Accordingly, we turn to inspect some of Royce's marginalia and then to add brief comments which we hope will shed additional light on his letter to James.

When Martineau wrote about the "underlying continuum of Time," Royce jotted: "Both K[ant] and M. are not sufficiently aware that time is at the start no continuum at all." Soon when Martineau asserted, "Kant allows that self-knowledge at least is possible," Royce noted down the qualification: "But only knowledge of present self."[22]

Royce here reasserted the limited starting point he had already employed for a decade—namely, the present self in its self-knowledge. In this self is the start of time, a start that is deeper than continuity and therefore somehow prior to it, more real than it, and thus more valuable than it. By thinking philosophically, Royce had now made himself reflectively present to "the vital issue of every moment"—the issue of which he was concomitantly conscious during his nonreflective moments. This issue was how the now-actual self, present to its preconscious and conscious life-flow (with all its biological, psychological, and spiritual activities and passivities), is called to handle and actually does handle this life-flow. At this depth, the self's finite freedom is the origin of time, and hence of continuity.[23] Already Royce's dark "trouble with Continuity" (with its world of description and causation) is paradoxically "enlightening . . . the whole range of metaphysics" (with its world of freely appreciative selves). As mentioned, after making these notes, Royce soon encountered Martineau's exposition and critique of *The Religious Aspect of Philosophy*.

When Martineau thereafter treated theism according to "Explicit and Implicit Will," Royce wrote in the margin: "The determinating [*sic*] character of a cause as choosing this from that requires the cause to be true volition as distinct from blind power."[24] By requiring that a "choosing cause" have a true volition to determine its choice soundly, under pain of otherwise becoming a blind power, Royce put the present choosing self into the genuine appreciative world and not into the morally evil world of untrue volitions. But his requirement of truth to guide the present self's volition implicitly raised the question whether it can get truth of itself or needs some other or others to attain truth.

A dozen pages later, when Martineau criticized Theodore Parker's abstract Infinite, Royce noted: "M's answer to Parker is that the Infinite, far from being the abstract total, is for us the Alter Ego of the finite."[25] Like Martineau's recent critique of Royce's "Universal Thought" as a do-nothing and a "negation of will," this critique of Parker's "abstract total Infinite" moved Royce to concretize and enliven his Logos by getting into intersubjective relation with it, as "Alter Ego."[26]

Whatever the factual connections of Martineau's texts with Royce's insights, by thinking of the Infinite as the Alter Ego of the finite, Royce here placed himself in a concrete intersubjective universe. The Infinite Alter Ego is viewed as a superhuman personal Subject, different from each finite self, yet being the ultimate center of identification for each self since the latter regards the Infinite Alter Ego as its own Other Self. Interestingly, this relationship to the Infinite Alter Ego runs through the whole human community as a real, nonindividual, shared life that mediates between every member and the Infinite Alter Ego. After criticizing Martineau for not appreciating social consciousness, Royce raised a characteristic question: "Is it not then the social rather than the individual conscience which is objective and the road towards the divine?"[27] The finite, individual, moral conscience needs to undergo the demands of the human community in order to achieve objectivity and a resultant orientation to the divine Alter Ego. Royce viewed such a "Theocratic conception of Society" sounder than Martineau's. For the free judgment of each finite self is impossible without a call-to-the-other— both to the human others in community and to the Infinite Other. This radical call, or appeal, became a key intersubjective aspect of Royce's later philosophy.[28]

But was this discovery of intersubjectivity, of a free call (and response) operative in each judgment, the deepest thought to which Royce came during his 1888 cruise? Having a sense for reality's complexity, Royce saw that the more experiential norm of human and divine intersubjectivity itself needed to be constantly steadied by an anchoring norm intrinsic to Being. After a few pages, he jotted his most metaphysical note. Our strategic estimate of its importance is confirmed by the sleuthing of a master researcher, Ralph Barton Perry. He, too, evidently tracked Royce back to his marginalia on Martineau's *A Study of Religion*.[29] On encountering the present metaphysical gem, Perry made it, as far as I can determine, the only specimen he lifted out by hand-copy from Royce's marginalia. Perry's selection suggests that he discovered here the bright carat-value he cherished. Undoubtedly it is the clearest statement we have of Royce's metaphysical position on his 1888 cruise. It gives additional depth and sparkle to his 1885 starting point and theistic argument. Such a key text calls for special study.

Royce avowed to James that the "trouble about Continuity" seemed particularly enlightening "for our question about Freedom and the Ideals." In the text that follows, although only "Freedom" is mentioned explicitly, "Continuity" and the "Ideals" operate so near the surface that the text seems to give a clear picture of how Royce then viewed all three. I regard it as the closest we can come to the basis of

Royce's "metaphysical speculation" of 1888. Along Martineau's margin, Royce's hand etched all the following emphases, dashes, parentheses, and brackets—in an abundance unusual even for Royce—as he wrote:

If nothing be clearer than that the true Knower must include his known object [and this principle I conceive to be absolutely true], then God as all-Knower, must include *us*. How our agency is saved in such a world, is another and a later question. But Freedom and Agency must simply take care of themselves until the conditions of Knowing (which are the conditions constitutive of Being) are saved and satisfied to the full. —For M. the consciousness of agency is the beginning of wisdom, and its demands must be first met. For me it is knowledge as such that is the first datum of all Thinking— —A finite knowledge as such being self-contradictory, *therefore* (as I conceive) must the true subject be the Infinite All-Knower, and thus the all-includer. Agency and causation find their due place *in* and *for* this Knower.[30]

In this text I find: 1) a *par excellence* sense of truth, knowledge, and being; 2) a settling of basic metaphysical options for Royce; 3) a clear instance of how Royce philosophized through conceptions and inferences; and 4) a concrete theistic termination of his inference to an Infinite All-Knowing Self. Some exposition of these four aspects of the Roycean text seems in order.

In the phrases "true Knower" and "true subject," Royce significantly uses "true" to point to a *par excellence* meaning, that is, to a teleological sense of the ultimately genuine and real. For him, finite knowing is always less than fully true, and is always done by a self or subject not standing fully in himself. Accordingly, the text reveals which ideals operate here and how they operate. The "genuinely true" is envisioned as a key ideal, and implicitly opposed to the erroneous and even to whatever is not yet fully true. All-inclusive unity is another ideal functioning in contrast to the fragmentation which leaves some elements totally unrelated. "Being" functions in contrast to the unreal.

Moreover, "freedom" and "agency"are clearly given a reduced priority. So, the fullest Knowing, Being, and Unity are Royce's chosen triad of basic ideals. They are seen to operate in a *par excellence* way, so that all finite knowing, being, and unity can get their value only through teleological identification with the Infinite Knower. As Subject, he is the goal for these objects of his knowing. As Infinite Self, he is the inescapable norm for all ministerial selves in their finite freedom and agency—a matter that another marginal note clarifies.[31]

According to this central Roycean text, man in his quest for wisdom is confronted with the radical option of starting either from the consciousness of agency, as Martineau did, or from knowledge as such, as Royce judged the wiser course. Knowledge as such leads him to make the crucial distinction between the Infinite Knower and finite knowers. To try to think of a finite knower simply as such is to attempt the inconceivable, for finite knowers and doers unavoidably "are at once the objects and ministers of [Infinite] Thought."[32] Of all knowers the latter alone has no "object just beyond" and no "subject just below." Into the basis of his metaphysical speculation, Royce built several radical choices. Not only did he prefer knowledge as such to agency, in contrast to Martineau. He also preferred to make the conditions of knowing be the conditions constitutive of Being. So at least for us, as human knowers and beings, knowledge has a constitutive priority over Being, and subjectivity has a priority over objectivity, even though in both pairs either pole implies the other.

This key marginal comment further displays how Royce did his philosophy through true conceptions and the inferences they generate. More obviously, it shows him opting for a particular starting point from which he will infer an order of questions. The basic initial conception he explores here is that of true Knower. And as seen, he ultimately finds finite knowledge as such inconceivable.

Royce's early "then . . . must," and his emphasized "*therefore* . . . must" near the close of this notation, reflect his commitment to develop wisdom by reasoning out implications from some maximally clear starting point. Since "knowledge as such is the first datum of all Thinking," it won Royce's acceptance as his starting point. From this he needed to find and maintain an order of metaphysical questions without violating his system of all-inclusive unity. Through the inclusiveness of the true Knower everything is internally related to everything else. Because Royce united this internal relationship with his posited priority of Knowing-Being, he had to relegate freedom and agency to a secondary rank.

Royce's inference moved necessarily beyond finitude to its theistic term, the Infinite All-Knower, who is here identified with God insofar as he is related to us by his knowledge. When Royce touched here the all-inclusive Divine Knower, he reached ultimate concreteness in his metaphysics. For the Infinite All-Knower must include himself as object and thus constitute himself a Divine Self.

It would take Royce decades to work out the unique individuations of the Divine Self and of ourselves in their reciprocity. Yet, this text reveals in seminal form the relationship between the Infinite Self and finite selves. In time it would germinate as the living root of his *Conception of God* (1897) and *The World and the Individual* (1899-1901). Yet already in 1888, the way Royce perceived his new "metaphysical speculation"—a way he readily shared with James— was that it had more power than any previous conception of his to make live the "dry bones" of his Universal Thought.

It is noteworthy that Royce experienced his speculative contact with this Infinite Alter Ego, or Knower inclusive of us, or Divine Self, as *most enlivening* and so shared it with James. He thus revealed his valuation of life and its Source. That giving of life which is based on knowing now functioned as a key value in Royce's speculation and as a root of his World of Appreciation. True, he did not here use the term "divine living Self." But its Reality operated as the control of the metaphysical order which Royce clearly set down here: first and deepest, the Infinite True Knower of all; secondly, the world of finite, not-fully-true knowers; and thirdly, the world of physical causation among objects which we view as nonknowing. Upon this basic order he built his 1892 distinction between the Worlds of Appreciation and Description.

In the central marginal note just discussed, Royce put knowledge before freedom and valued the lived relationships between concrete selves (finite and infinite) more than the "dry bones" of abstract universals. Now, as he entered Martineau's chapter on determinism and free will, what pressed in on him, to judge from his notes, was the problem of uniting knowledge with freedom—that is, of synthesizing speculative truth with practical self-commitment in community. Speculatively, the thought of a finite thinker included the Infinite Knower. But Royce's practical experience of himself in moral agency made him confess his sense of being companioned, his uncertainty about the identity of the agent or agents responsible, and his humble sense of hope in some divine presence and leadership at work in his moral efforts. In such notes he moved along Martineau's main line that God is "ruling the universe and holding moral relations with mankind,"[33] but at the same time Royce repudiated Martineau's assumption that as individuals we are *wholly* autonomous agents.

For example, Martineau proposed that his own awareness of commanding his lower self (with its emotions and inclinations) was evidence enough for recognizing himself as one and the same as the agent who exercised freedom in this command. Summing up his view, Martineau wrote, "I submit that the consciousness of self, as an identical personality, is the consciousness of such power [of freely commanding one's feelings]."[34] To this, Royce countered:

But consciousness *is* not a sufficient witness in me to such a power. God knows, not I, if I be such.

Those who base my freedom on the mere fact of my moral consciousness, forget that this consciousness is essentially *critical*. It can say what one ought to do *if* he is a moral agent. This it says alike of Paul, or of Hamlet, or of myself. But that Paul *is* a moral agent I know not, for perhaps Christ works *in* him. That Hamlet is *not* such an agent I know, because he does not exist save as a poetic creation. Even so however, I myself, as moral critic, know not whether I can do so and so, but only that whoever works in me is responsible. . . .

That *somebody* is at work here in me is not only my irresistible impression, but is a philosophically justifiable notion. But *who* it is I cannot tell. My heart is too little mine to know. I can only hope.[35]

As mentioned, Royce's mind has fittingly been described as "trying to control a bursting complexity of thought."[36] The confession in this marginal notation reveals an authentic dimension of his mind much less well known than his commitment to a priority for knowledge which the immediately preceding marginal comment manifested. Hence, this latest marginal note needs a close study.

First, Royce wrote that when he critically examined his consciousness of commanding his own feelings, he did not find enough evidence to declare that the power of freedom was solely his own. Within his experience of controlling his feelings, his agnosticism did not have as its target *whether* some moral agent was operating. Of that he was sure. But he focused on his own inability, as a finite knower, to identify certainly *which* of the several selves within Royce was or were responsible for this control of his feelings. First, there was the divine Alter Ego of which he wrote. Secondly, a few pages later Royce would write of a "sinner self": "I find myself a sinner in my first moment of moral consciousness."[37] In the present marginal notation, his lines echoed chapters 7 and 8 of Paul's letter to the Romans with its plurality of selves.

Other "inner selves," at which Royce had earlier hinted, and to which he soon would draw public attention in his 1894 "Meister Eckhart" article, almost certainly complicated Royce's problem of identification here.[38] For included among Royce's "many selves" were his bodily self, with its "powers" of reasoning, planning, and deciding; his ideal self, which he hoped to bring to realization; and his *Fünkelin* self—that uncreated spark in Royce which was God's living idea of Royce. Little wonder, then, that he could not discern within such mysterious depths exactly which self was active in his moral deed.

At the start of the last paragraph in this marginal notation, Royce acknowledged undergoing an "irresistible impression" that somebody was at work in him, without being able to tell certainly who it was. If he were in an ordinary psychic state when he wrote this, he was an unusually acute discerner of his own ordinary states. But his "irresistible impression" that an unidentified somebody was at work suggests rather that he was then undergoing a "peak experience"—something his letter to James corroborates. When a person is in a "peak experience," a creative energy inside him apparently possesses and directs him rather than he directing it. This leads him easily to wonder whether he is not really the more passive, yet cooperative, instrument of some higher creative self at work within himself. Royce here found that his moral agency had this mysterious unidentifiability at its roots. Accordingly, lover of clarity that he was, he placed moral agency in a metaphysical position secondary to knowledge as such, his first datum of thinking, by which he could identify this creative agency.

In the same paragraph, after describing his "irresistible impression," Royce went on to assert that philosophy can validate the notion of such an unidentified agency. Here his mind hovered because its one certainty was surrounded by correlative ignorances. For he knew someone was acting—a knowledge he found validated by his present "irresistible impression." Yet, as he confronted the mysteries of his own (or other's) individuality and of the identifiability of individual selves, he also experientially knew his ignorances.

How characteristic of Royce was his next line, "My heart is too little mine to know. I can only hope." Though he was at his own center (indicated by his use of "my heart" in the usual biblical sense), still he confessed feeling the limits of his own self-knowledge. Yet instead of allowing this uncertainty and mystery to draw him into a despair of knowing, he interpreted whatever was going on in his heart as being somehow worthwhile and calling for hope. Here Royce overcame his lack of knowledge through his Pauline hope that somehow he was a genuine moral agent and, further, that indeed a higher moral agent was working in and through him.

Besides this blend of knowledge with ignorance and of uncertainty with hope, the passage shows Royce's critical acumen. He asserted here the need for a more critical posture than Martineau displayed when the latter inferentially identified his own selfhood from the experience of his power to command. Royce refrained from inferentially declaring the moral agent to be one wholly autonomous self. He neither affirmed nor denied that some other was working in him and with him. Thus, almost a decade before his 1896 insight into individuality, Royce already manifested how hard the question of the identifiability of a unique individual pressed him.[39]

Finally, Royce critically adopted here the attitude neither of an ontologist nor of a naturalist. For whatever the self was, it was not some wholly unrelated *Ding-an-sich* that ontologists claim to know, nor any of those self-sufficient substances they construct. On the other hand, he did not start off by ruling out all nonnatural "preexistent reals"—a hasty methodological exclusion which naturalists demand in advance.[40] Avoiding both kinds of pretensions, Royce kept his mind open to a possible cooperation with moral agents in an unseen world. But he regarded these as objects, not of knowledge, but of hope.

In the marginal note just studied, Royce was implicitly testing his "metaphysical speculation." Would it stand up against the problem of evil already experienced in his own ignorance about moral agency? In other words, could the All-Knower, as the basis of Royce's "metaphysical speculation," include all moral agents, despite all their finite ignorance? Now Royce let the full force of the problem of evil supply the supreme testing of his "metaphysical speculation": Could the All-Knower maintain unity in the moral order even while permitting the deepest moral evil? For, as Royce had noted in his key text, "Agency and causation find their due place *in* and *for* this Knower." Thus, he now asked whether a moral universe can be preserved if finite selves are agents of moral evil and even "cause another to sin."

Even though the Infinite Seer's speculative knowledge did not suffice to build the sort of unity needed in a moral universe, would his practical Self-Knowledge provide the basic unity needed to allow and yet contain such a permissive sweep to moral evil? For such Self-Knowledge freely committed itself to its chosen ideals and then embodied them in each finite self's "immediate vital issue of every moment." In two marginalia on the problem of evil, Royce developed his argument. He moved no longer simply through the possibility of (speculative) error, but now through the moral permissibility of an inborn finite hostility toward the Infinite Appreciator.

While reading Martineau's chapter on moral evil, Royce wrote in the margin:

Here is the difficulty which M. declines to face fully and fairly, in this discussion; *viz.*, the difficulty that, in a moral world, one free agent should be permitted to cause another not merely to suffer, but to sin, to be morally degraded. For it is in and through the resulting moral degradation and crime of the victims that persecution and slave-making show their truly evil character. The physical suffering that they cause is not their greatest fault. This difficulty not only has a solution, but embodies the true solution of the whole business. Mr. M. slights it.[41]

Royce discerned that "the true solution of the whole business" lay within this difficulty which Martineau had failed to face. Royce's response here ran parallel to his characteristic way of penetrating the possibility of error in order to recognize the Unerring Knower. "The bone in his throat" with which he now struggled was "that, in a moral world, one free agent should be permitted to cause another . . . to sin." How could this be for the better? For, if permitted evil were not for the better, then our moral world, where such factual permission operates, is for the worse. Ultimately, there would be total moral disorder and life would be radically absurd.

Royce countered such irrationalism with a "true solution," namely, that indispensable condition which warrants permitting a finite self to mislead another morally. For if somebody is at work within a finite self's moral agency, the somebody must include a practically committed Infinite Appreciator of certain ideals. This All-Knower freely wants to express these ideals both by himself and by a community of finite instrumental selves working according to their limitations in knowledge and freedom. Without the directive presence of such an Appreciator of ideals (who is also Operative Director of their realization in the moral universe and Effective Restorer of finite fragmentations in that universe) both the misleading and the misled finite selves would ultimately be living in a universe invalidly normed—that is, in a chaotic, absurd universe. But the factual permission of such moral evil—for example, when parents transmit inborn vicious inclinations to their children—entails the factual establishment of its correlative moral good as norm. But this, in turn, requires an Infinite Appreciator who keeps all finite moral agents in a highly pluralistic but ultimately unified moral universe.

Later on, when Martineau treated the psychology of voluntary action, Royce wrote a long marginal comment on a kind of original sin which fate causes to be transmitted to us. Royce's previous concern—how does such causation find its due place in and for such a Knower—seems the context within which he jotted:

This doctrine, (that my sinfulness of character, even if I did not make it, but another, still in part condemns me), must be admitted by even the partisans of free-will. For there is a doubleness about the consciousness of sin that Paul first stated. I *find* myself a sinner in the first moment of my moral consciousness. This is the truth of original sin. But then I find, when I go wrong afterwards, that I now sin in the light and afresh. The first or original sin, my selfish love of freedom, is inborn, and so not free. It is my proper but pre-destined viciousness of heart. With this burden aboard I must fight. My second sin, my yielding, *may* be free or not. If it is free, then indeed I am a moral agent, with a second and graver load of blame on me. But unless I could first sin by fate, the moral world would have no gravity. For then one agent could not "cause an-other to sin," say as by begetting a vicious son.[42]

One of Royce's most profound and perilous insights lies in this text. When he confessed, "I *find* myself a sinner in the first moment of my moral consciousness," he manifested more than an experience of inner deviancy countered by the moral "ought." For as sinner (and not mere nonconformist), Royce found himself "in part condemned" (judged not completely right) by God, the Infinite Alter Ego and Ap-preciator. His felt alienation from the All-Holy exposed a profound dimension in Royce's moral consciousness—a di-mension disregarded by most current ethicians of perfect autonomy. Yet his deep insight also verges on the dangerous, although his "in part" may save this idea. For here Royce did not connect his insight with the love, mercy, and healing of the Divine Appreciator, as decades later he would explicitly do in his *Problem of Christianity*.[43]

In the two final sentences of this last marginal notation, Royce again manifested his concern with the problem, "In a moral universe, how *may* the causal transmission of an evil tendency be permitted?" How *may* a hostile inclination of will towards God be allowed to be transmitted, for example, in the begetting of a vicious son, when, by this inclination, the recipient will be judged to stand partly in the wrong even before making his first free choice? At stake here for Royce was the saving of the unity of his moral universe. In 1888 Royce wrote only a sketchy reply to this question.[44]

To sum up, by employing six selected sets of marginalia to illuminate Royce's letter to James, we hope to have gained a better context and greater accuracy for interpreting how Royce had "largely straightened out the big metaphysical tangle about continuity, freedom, and the world-formula." Having witnessed how his "very simple . . . metaphysical speculation" through its World of Appreciation illumined his question about freedom and the ideals, we now turn to see the very expansive nature of this key speculation. Did it already enable Royce to recognize the loyal self? And how would it affect his interpretation of social and political institutions in Australia and America?

4

Ethics
of
Loyalty

Soon after his August 1888 landing in California, Royce reported to William James, "The colonies are charming studies in human nature and politics, and I return feeling much older and wiser—not to add, immensely happier."[1] Royce felt wiser because by now he had grasped how central to the ethical life is faithfulness (or loyalty) and because he had already rather fully articulated this principle. I base this conservatively stated, though perhaps surprising, claim on his 1888-1889 writings as compared with his much later *Philosophy of Loyalty* (1907).

Royce had reported that his new "metaphysical speculation" particularly illuminated the "question about Freedom and the Ideals."[2] Evidently, this special light was at work in Royce's 1888 writings where his ideas on loyalty clearly emerged as individual threads but not yet as a total fabric. Therefore, to guide our survey of texts, we, rather than Royce, interweave his threads of 1888 to sum up loyalty as: a "homeseeking devotion" whereby one freely commits oneself to a concrete historical community and subordinates one-self socially in a nonindividualistic way to "the ideal of a good order" with a "cheerful conformity to the general will of the community."[3]

To test whether Royce had already in 1888-1891 a rather full grasp of loyalty, we will first study what traits emerged in his descriptions of the Australians' loyalty to social institutions. We will then examine his sketch of the loyal backwoodsman whom Royce discovered on his return voyage to San Francisco and whom he soon portrayed for *Atlantic Monthly* readers with more than usual care and interest. However, to appreciate these two tests, we need a brief introduction to our textual sources, to Royce as ethician, and to the role of loyalty within any ethical enterprise.

Our perhaps surprising claim that Royce already had a good grasp of loyalty in 1888 is based mainly on Royce's long article, "Reflections after a Wandering Life in Australasia" (which occupied two issues of the *Atlantic*), and on his appraisal of this article found in a letter to Alfred Deakin.[4] He looked on his "Reflections" as "the first fruit of my journey." Modestly and humorously he described the article to Deakin as "all . . . very superficial," as "addressed to the blind by a one-eyed man," and as "the usual omniscient observations which travellers make on a society that they have not had time to see." Although Royce has justly confessed his status as a nonexpert in Australian affairs, yet his meaning of "very superficial" needs to be measured. If this "superficial" is gauged by his easy familiarity with the depths of metaphysics, such as we recently noticed in the central marginal note he penned on Martineau—the note that caught R. B. Perry's eye —then, Royce rightly regarded these articles as "very superficial." Yet their lighter tone fortunately allowed other aspects of Royce's personality to surface, including, it seems, his intellectual growth along ethical and political lines—even though Royce considers himself a novice author on Australasia who is writing in a popular, nonethical genre for the *Atlantic*'s average reader.

With these warnings in mind, we should also note that in 1888 Royce did not have to contend with the negative connotations that the term "loyalty" evokes today in some persons. To avoid some of these current connotations, we rely, at least partially, on Royce's initial terms: "faithfulness" and "having faith in the value of faithfulness." Such usage and all his remarks about faithfulness (or loyalty) in his "Reflections" preceded by almost twenty years his popular *Philosophy of Loyalty* (1907). Yet even before expressing his 1888 grasp of faithfulness, Royce had already, since completing his doctoral studies, twice taught ethics at Harvard, published three major works on ethical themes, and authored half a dozen articles on ethics.[5] Furthermore, from his earliest boyhood writings, he had shown a keen, persistent interest in ethical questions.

In view of these facts, clearly the Royce of the 1888 cruise was familiar with, and sensitive to, the basic problems and tensions of ethics. He acknowledged that during this cruise he focused on "an immediate vital issue of every moment," on "a burning problem of life." It is hardly coincidental, then, that the ethician Royce should, within a few months, write of never "losing faith in the value of faithfulness."[6] Here he clearly foreshadowed his later 1907 theme, "Be loyal to loyalty."

The ethically experienced Royce of 1888 was familiar, then, with the central questions of ethical life concerning faithfulness. How does an individual coordinate a fitting independence with the constructive obedience required by his basic social ties? How does a person keep his loyalty from arising mainly out of spontaneous feelings rather than out of a synthesis of courageous intelligence with his feelings? Can loyalty permit intelligence to be sufficiently critical? Can it support courage for persistently countering the alienating forces at work both inside and outside the individual? How can one forestall a degradation of loyalty into an impractical romantic embrace of all men and all noble causes? How does loyal inquiry and commitment generate practical and determinate guidance? Do we occasionally need to show some "unfaithfulness" toward those persons who display a habitual lack of fidelity? Can loyalty heal selves of the alienations that develop toward institutions and authority figures? If so, how is this healing achieved—especially when the fallibility and moral failures of institutions and leaders become clear?

Such an orientation turns us now to Royce's own "Reflections" for the beginning of his answers to these questions. Royce's 1888 expressions about loyalty were occasioned by the Australians' tendency to organize their social life highly, especially in its nonpolitical areas. In these "Reflections," he repeatedly uses the term "loyalty" and often implicitly refers to its reality. For example, when generalizing from the Australians' attitude towards social institutions as the instruments of their organized communal life, Royce wrote, "Organization, if it succeeds, does so by virtue of the loyalty of the individuals, and the result must be in general normal and progressive."[7] As root gives rise to stem and flower, so, according to Royce, the faithfulness of individuals gives rise to successful organization and thereby to the positive development of society.

He contrasted the loyal Australian way with the "decidedly individualistic," and therefore nonloyal, way of most Americans, who exaggerated the emphasis Emerson placed on self-reliance and independence and mistakenly imbibed as much of the "philosophy of the sacredness of broken ties as our sound English common sense would permit us to do." He continued his appraisal: "In consequence, we have (not indeed by Emerson's authority) often cultivated flippancy for the sake of not seeming to ourselves too submissive to order and to social bondage, and have preferred to be rebellious in our lives, even if we had to give ourselves the strain and wear that lonesome individualism always brings with itself." Yet any intelligent person, even while alert to the ever-present sins and failings of evolving human organizations, should, according to Royce, believe that such organized enterprises are the beginnings of a higher social order.[8] But the bias of many Americans unfortunately drives them to denounce as monopoly or as foreign oppression any enterprise that capitalists or trade unions organize. Meanwhile, through their own "capricious competition," they waste much effort. In addition, through their political unconcern, Americans suffer from an apathy that enervates the United States. All this weakens the concrete reasonableness of loyalty.

But in Australia, "from the outset, such individualism is subordinated." For unlike the typical American, the Australian "has inherited an immense respect for the social order in his own way." The components of this order are social institutions, "our own creatures, our most powerful servants." Despite their flaws and partial abuses, we find in them our destiny. For this reason we watch closely the Australians, who, in Royce's eyes, were characteristically loyal to social institutions.

In Royce's "Reflections," what signs reveal this loyalty of the Australians? When I reply that there are a dozen such signs, the reader deserves a methodological caution. The following marks of loyalty derive substantially from the 1888 mind of Royce found in his Australasian writings, although I am responsible for their ordering. Because I may at first appear hypersensitive to principles of loyalty in Royce's writings, an analogy may clarify my position. A person trained in reading fetal photographs may warrantably speak of an "eye-bud" or "earbud" at certain spots where the ordinary observer detects only the slightest folds of skin. Similarly, the loci offered for the twelve following "marks of loyalty" in the 1888 Royce may at first appear only as explicit as "mere folds of skin."

But let us begin our search for marks of loyalty by recalling how impressed Royce was by the success with which the Australians usually balanced their sense of personal freedom and their serious recognition of the social order. One of the many factors entering into this balance was their recognition of a common heritage, home, and history. We may take, then, as a first mark of loyalty *a shared sense of common bonds as already experienced.*

Independent through their geographical and historical isolation, the Australians still remained tied in many ways to their heritage of British civilization. They also had a common sense of their great continent as a basic life-source and as a challenge for all. Furthermore, they shared jointly in their common past history; they sensed how their present condition depended on the deeds and dedication of the earlier frontiersmen, settlers, miners, and government officials.[9] Moreover, Royce later described the elder Australians as "generally loyal to tradition; lovers often of the Church of their fathers . . . faithful to the mother-country, proud of the British connection."[10] Such was their shared sense of common roots in the past.

Secondly, their loyalty was marked by *a shared sense of a concrete common hope.* Some Australians "carried about . . . the ideal of a good order," to be realized in their shared life and land.[11] As a common task their coastal slopes, rugged mountains, and formidable desert challenged them continuously. Most of them, according to Royce, also hoped for an eventual federation of their colonies into one nation. Such hopes, setting a healthy idealism aglow in the Australians, were preserved from a vain romanticism by a business sense that disciplined these hopes into practical deeds.

Besides a feeling for their common past and common hopes, the Australians possessed a third ingredient of loyalty, one already mentioned and one that steadied them in the present—namely, an *"immense respect for the social order itself."* They saw how large and complex was the social order developing in their land and consequently, according to Royce, showed "a degree of conservatism." Thus, although they cherished their own forms of personal private liberty, the Australians demonstrated "a great love for social ties," both interpersonal and institutional. Rooted in a faith in the value of faithfulness itself, this conservative love tended to bring their common ideals and purposes to further realization.[12]

It becomes obvious, then, why their faith embodied itself in shared agreements about the future cooperative deeds which they pledged to, and expected of, one another. "After all," Royce soon asked, "are not social ties the glory of rational human life?"[13] At the individual level, such mutual agreements materialized in the social ties of contracts and covenants; at the provincial level, in confederation agreements, then under way; and at the international level, "in sharing the ideals and work of humanity" in practical ways that eventually would achieve legal form. Royce offered examples of other "institutionalized social ties" that the Australians loved: trade unions, new commercial and cultural enterprises, extensive leagues of amateur sports, municipal systems for street building and refuse removal, and socially alert newspapers. The elaborate social order in Australia was something calling for immense respect, for some conservatism, and for an avoidance of flippancy. As a balance against those eager for quick, drastic legislative changes, Royce pointed to "such a wealth of political duties as forces a community to move deliberately and cautiously."[14]

Fourthly, the Australians' loyalty showed "*a degree . . . of public spirit,*" an awareness of belonging to a group life greater than one's private life. As an example of such responsibility to the community Royce instanced the Australian press as generally far more alert to its role than American papers, for it provided a balanced account of news and issues, mediated through a more critically refined editorial judgment.[15] The inner thrust of loyalty tended to lift one out of his narrowly private interests. If Americans were more public-spirited, they would recognize the basically good roots of social evolution in the nation's best efforts at organized freedom. If so, they would not immediately tend to condemn the formation of a trade union or the merger of businesses as something hostile, but would recognize such a step as a symbol of their own best interests.

Forestalling an inherited rebelliousness against the social order and against a public spirit responsible for this order, Royce mentioned "*a degree . . . of social discipline.*" We can take this as a fifth mark of loyalty. If the group's basic cooperative needs are to be achieved, it needs to discipline its members by approval or disapproval. Twenty-two years earlier, at Lincoln Grammar School in San Francisco, about a thousand boys had, in an "impressively disciplinary and persistent" way, introduced a quaint, countrified lad called Josiah to the demands of their group consensus—or, as he later phrased it, to the "majesty of the community."[16] Now he appreciated how the Australians both expected and accepted strong government action promptly exercised in time of urgent needs and crises. From their youth they were trained to the social discipline needed to maintain and advance the social order. Perhaps one had served as a crewman on a ship and another as a member of a sporting team; thus each learned the need for disciplined cooperative actions if the group was to survive decently.

Sixthly, loyalty is marked by *"a degree . . . of cheerful conformity to the general will of the community."* For a community to exist and to secure basic cooperation, a consensus on certain fundamental values has to be achieved. Royce found that the Australians had created more than a minimal consensus, thanks mainly to their common heritage. Their membership in the British Empire "exists by virtue of a general good-will and because it is at present the most convenient fashion of life for all parties."[17] So any calls for immediate independence were simply rash.

He also discovered during his stay there that on the occasion of the Chinese agitation, the "Australian public was of one mind that Chinese immigration must be discouraged.[18] Such uniformity of the Australian general will did not operate solely upon minority groups inside Australia to evoke their basic conformity to the majority; like all expressions of a community's general will, it also called upon outside groups —the British government, other colonies, other nations—respectfully to recognize its consensus. "Downing Street" and the Chinese nation should respectfully recognize this general will.

Not incidentally, Royce required that this conformity be cheerful. For both loyalty and the community were in trouble when the basic pleasantness seeped out of social cooperation, and especially when the needed conformity was only reluctantly offered or even coercively imposed—as had happened to the pro-Chinese groups in the recent agitation. In Royce's sense of loyalty, a bored or bitter spirit did not qualify.

On the other hand, as we saw, Royce thought some Americans lacked a degree of conformity to the genuine will of their nation. For in the emergent forms of organized enterprise, they failed to recognize genuine expressions of their

own best interests, the "beginnings of a higher social order."
Perceptible abuses in some enterprises and the American heritage of rebelliousness led to this partial blindness. Hence, many Americans often disloyally tended to disassociate themselves from social endeavors which by organizing their freedom aimed to carry out the people's general will. On this point, Royce found the Australians more loyal.

If one is to take part in the community's general will, an indispensable step is *to adopt a cause in common*. Already in 1888, Royce used the term "cause" to refer to the objective of loyalty. This came close to his 1907 meaning of an objective superindividual value, personally treasured and served.[19] He wrote popularly of Englishmen on holiday who often display a common readiness "to speak for a noble cause." Yet causes were more than topics for picnics, for achievement of the ideal events of our hopes is usually attained through nonholiday situations. Royce found at Sydney, for instance, some leaders from Victoria who belonged to a "union intended to promote the cause of the federation of the colonies."[20] Their cause of federation served as a dynamic interest that united and strengthened them, especially in confronting the colonial dangers of excessive provincialism and of too-hasty, overactive, political organization. Royce found "the chief hope of Australia must lie in the federation of her now disunited communities." Beyond federation, he saw the lure of eventual independence from Britain emerging as a cause. This would happen because of Australia's unique calling in the South Pacific. Moreover, Royce found that the Australian backwoodsman of his return trip to San Francisco had never lost "faith in the value of faithfulness" and that this was the cause to which the man dedicated "his courageous idealism."[21] By adopting such a cause, his friend entered the community of those holding the moral insight—or, as is said today, "the moral point of view."

Adopting an order of preference for settling conflicts of loyalty is an eighth mark of loyalty. Already in 1888, Royce was settling future conflicts of loyalty.[22] He then faced the issue that in the not too distant future the question of Chinese immigration would make the Australians' loyalty to their own national development conflict with their loyalty to the British Empire. In such a situation, he recommended that the Australians terminate their empire connection in a firm and friendly way. For both communities, he said, "will serve humanity best by parting company, not in enmity, but in faithful pursuit of their very different callings." With all men they shared the common cause of humanity. With other members of the empire, they shared the common cause of British commerce and civilization. But for the Australians, their own people was a common cause that called for deeper attachment than did the imperial cause. For though numerically larger, the empire was only a cultural politicoeconomic organization, not a people. Accordingly, Royce wrote, "The deeper loyalty of the Australian must always be to his own people." Royce's order of preference placed primacy on a fitting loyalty to oneself and one's unique calling within one's own people and its calling. He closed his "Refections" reemphasizing this point: "We all work best abroad when we first possess our own homes in peace."[23] So Royce's loyalty possessed a healthy pragmatism through its use of this order of preference. Thus he evaluated causes for their priorities within decision making and he forestalled any tendency merely to gaze at starry ideals.

Loyalty is also marked by *courage and patience in the struggle and striving* that devoted service requires. Very characteristically Royce highlighted the endurance and bravery of the Australian frontiersman struggling against the desert. He also clearly admired the sense of skillful contest shown by Deakin and other governmental officials—provided that they acted as genuinely responsible ministers of the people and not as mere managers seeking their own ends. He treasured any Australian who was "loyally disposed to rear . . . the ideal of a good order" amid indifferent or even hostile persons. Amid disorderly feelings and forces, loyalty called for a patient, courageous maintenance and development not only of moral order in the individual but also of political order in organized society.[24]

Royce touched on another mark of loyalty: *the balancing role of justice in our interactions with other communities.* In the work of world development, we are to do our share and make sure to balance what we take by what we give. Since this note strikes contemporary ears with special relevance, one wishes the 1888 Royce had developed the theme of justice. He did see that "to keep pace with the world's mental work" was a sine qua non for civilized development and that such pace-keeping requires of any nation that it be effectively fair when reaching out to other peoples and lands. Long before John Dewey made "interaction" the heart of his instrumentalism, Royce specifically mentioned the idea, without developing it: ". . . the true relation of foreign lands is one of interaction. When we do our share of the world's work, and give while we take, then only are we mentally alive."[25] With his "only" here, Royce inserted an exacting condition for being mentally alive. But he was convinced that one's duty in the world community required that each employ his time and talents well. Only if we will to "give while we take," can our interactions be fair and balanced.[26] In Royce's not fully articulated "will to work justice" in our interactions, we discern how far beyond mere sentiment he was. Sentiment may be part of Royce's 1888 grasp of loyalty, as when he wrote of the colonists' "mere sentiment of imperial loyalty [to the crown]."[27] But the operative demand upon oneself to contribute as much as one receives goes beyond sentiment. Thus, for example, if the crown required itself to contribute as much to the colonies' eventual independence as it demanded from them for its own welfare, then it would will the justice required by loyalty. Such a stress on balance in the intricate life of loyalty reveals itself, interestingly enough, in this and the two following traits of loyalty.

Balancing a catholicity of intent and of receptivity with a realistic sense of one's concrete limits is an eleventh mark of loyalty. On the one hand, loyalty requires a universalism of a generous intent towards all persons and a universalism of an accepting openness to various influences and ideas. Some Australians were rightly concerned for all the world's peoples. Yet others voiced the motto, "Australia for the Australians!" If they lived their motto in sheer exclusivism, Royce taught, these latter would eventually dehumanize themselves. For them the challenge was to interpret their motto open-endedly; that is, in "its true meaning, as implying also, 'and the Australians for mankind.' "[28]

Similarly, if they were to be influenced by the gifts of all peoples, the Australians needed a catholicity of receptivity. Indeed, Royce here found a necessary condition for effective freedom. For he thought it almost inevitable that for a long period, "the Australian youth will not care for that close intercourse with the world *which alone can make them freemen*" (emphasis added). Some Australians, unfortunately, tended to be excessively nationalistic, and "to feel indifferent towards all influences from other parts of the world." Expectably, Royce interpreted this lack of receptive catholicity as a philosopher would. He taught that the Australians particularly needed to be concerned with the whole course of modern thought in its broad spectrum. They should sharply counter "a provincial self-consciousness [that] will tend more and more to fight against the vast industry required to keep pace with the world's mental work."[29]

On the other hand, Royce balanced this universalism with a strong stress on local self-determination. In their practical priorities, the Australians needed to recognize their own unique destiny and concrete limits. Thus a reader of Royce, with head still echoing from the earlier idea of "the Australians for mankind," may be slightly jarred by his conclusion. For without opening the door to narrow provincialism, Royce inserted a significant "first of all claim" as he brought his "Reflections" to a close: ". . . our [Australian] brethren of the other hemisphere will serve all mankind by claiming first of all their Australia 'for the Australians.' "[30] That he favored their loyalty "beginning at home" is seen in his approval of tendencies towards local independence from Britain.[31] He nodded to the contention of the Queensland ministry that no governor should be appointed representing the crown unless he should previously have been discovered acceptable to the Australians. He was opposed to "Downing Street" making a final determination of Australian policy on the Chinese question. "In the long run," wrote Royce, "Australia must make its own Chinese policy, and the empire must conform thereto."[32] A so-called "Chinese Agitation" occurred during Royce's stay in Australia. He viewed it as a symbol of the need that all involved recognize the healthy instinct and justifiable and permanent sentiment of the Australian public.

Futhermore, if the Australians were to appreciate their own unique calling and destiny, they would have to attain a certain partial freedom from their traditions, heritage, and other outside influences. Since, in Royce's view, "the young Australian party" was "no doubt the beginning of the party of the future of Australia," Australians might for a while have to postpone studying the ideas of other peoples.[33] In such ways, then, Royce instanced his balancing of universalism and a realistic sense of authentic provincialism.

Finally, *loyalty requires the balance of independent self-reliance*, as Royce's sketch of his friendly backwoodsman, the "loyal and yet self-reliant character" will soon show. A corequisite for a faith in others is a fitting faith in oneself. This Roycean theme was already foreshadowed in his 1879 "Meditation before the Gate."[34] There Royce's self-dedication to philosophy was marked by earnestness, independence, and reverence. Similarly in "Reflections," the phrase "organized freedom" suggests the same paradoxical balance of a genuine independence and autonomy which is nonetheless directed by a community's presence and influence. When one commits oneself through loyalty to the common object of a cause, a self is stretched to something beyond his individualistic self and tied into a community of similar cointenders and coappreciators. On the other hand, only when a person comes into touch with his individual calling and destiny through autonomy and self-reliance can he fulfill the unique role he is to play in the community. Accordingly, the balance of the two corequisites is essential to the Roycean moral self of 1888.

In summary review, then, we have indicated a dozen characteristics of loyalty, as exemplified in Royce's descriptions of the Australians' attitude to social institutions. In 1888 he perceived the loyal self as having a shared sense of past common bonds and of concrete common hopes together with an immense respect for the social order. Because of this, the loyal self achieved a high degree of public spirit, of social discipline, and of cheerful conformity to the general will of the community. For these reasons the loyal self could adopt a common cause, determine an order of preference for settling conflicts of loyalty, cultivate courage and patience in the struggle, and develop a threefold dynamic to secure balance—of justice in our interactions, of catholicity with limitations, and of loyalty with self-reliance. I believe that in 1888 Royce explicitly articulated these twelve marks of loyalty or at least brought them so near the surface of expression that he provided clear hints about the direction his later doctrine on loyalty would take.

Accordingly, I see his 1888 view of loyalty as rather well developed. It already exhibited most of the ingredients proposed in his 1907 *Philosophy of Loyalty*, though it lacked many of the ingredients that emerged only in the transformed ethics of his final years.[35] Thanks to his transforming insight into Peirce, which began in 1912, Royce's maturest doctrine on loyalty (1915-1916) would operate on a new level. Logically, it would replace dyadic relations with triadic ones, use the *epsilon* relation to articulate itself, and by claiming fallibility, call for continuing efforts at reinterpretation. In content, it would exhibit a dialectic of estrangements and reconciliations, three kinds of estrangements and loyalties, and a paradoxical law (the greater union of selves occurs by way of their greater individualization). Surely, a second and later study is needed to validate the claims just made so apodictically. Meanwhile, however, may we simply indicate that many of his 1915-1916 insights into loyalty were not yet present in his 1888 view? Nor would they be present even in 1907. Nevertheless, this 1888-1891 articulation of loyalty contained most of the 1907 principles that would be used as the basis for the 1912-1916 advance to Royce's fullest philosophy of loyalty.

For Royce in 1888, however, loyalty was already more than a term with certain marks. When bonded with self-reliance, it meant authentic moral life. Steaming homeward on the *Alameda,* Royce met a man who almost personified loyalty. Royce portrayed this European who had pioneered in the backcountry of Australia as a "specimen of the true Australian bushman, of the more intellectual type," "an amusing and excellent fellow, Welch by name," "at heart he was a very good fellow, who could never knowingly utter a mean thing."[36] Hence, when Royce in his "Reflections" sought an authentic representative of the capacity and promise of the Australian nation, he turned to this frontiersman and man of the people, rather than to students or to literary writers.[37] Accordingly, to appreciate Royce's 1888 philosophic outline of the loyal yet fittingly independent self, we closely observe the cameo he drew when describing his blunt and vigorous companion on the *Alameda*.

Royce's unforgettable friend was a self-made man, "a good way past middle life, but still full of vigor and quick of wits." He had been "in early youth a naval officer," and "passed many years in the bush as explorer, adventurer, and country-newspaper editor." His was a life of continuous striving, of searching out survivors, and of fighting political battles. What Royce most noticed in him was his courageous idealism. He "had passed through all the bitterness of a long and hard life without ever losing faith in the value of faithfulness."[38] Such painful experiences taught him "he could not believe in many men; but he did believe in human life." He was one "who in youth had known the discipline of a quarterdeck and who had ever since carried about, in a faithless world, the ideal of a good order, which somehow nobody near him seemed to be loyally disposed to rear." In this text, a new aspect of Royce's 1888 view of the loyal self emerges. "The ideal of a good order" seems to refer more to the societal ideal of orderly cooperation for the common good than to one's personal ideal of a consistent life plan. Royce admired the self who constantly held on to such an ideal, who steadily carried it out, and who remained undaunted in raising this standard even when experiencing that many around him appeared uncommitted to the ideal. Moral excellence set one at odds with those ignoring, or even disbelieving, both the call and the demands of the common good. Such would be greedy businessmen or grossly selfish workingmen or venal politicians.

What Royce particularly admired in this backwoodsman was his intellectual questing and honesty. "He looked for signs of truth in his world as he would have looked for signs of distant water in the bush" was Royce's accurate description set in local color. The will to truth, so characteristic of Royce in the 1870s and 1880s, here became a basic and indispensable dynamism in the loyal self. This included an open honesty towards others which precludes such mask-wearing as hinders authenticity or alienates others. Royce saw that this frontiersman's "judgments were meanwhile all his own. . . . He was as honest a man as he was blunt." Finally, despite his open criticism of sham aristocrats and time-serving officials, the backwoodsman showed a true patriotism.

In brief, Royce confessed, "I found in him a more strongly defined, loyal, and yet self-reliant character than I had met on my travels for a long time." The unforgettable friend of the *Alameda* had created an outstanding moral balance by blending the independent use of his own resources with a committed faithfulness to his better self, his country, and his people. In this Australian Royce recognized the long-sought touchstone of his later ethics. His enlivened mind, having sketched out these lines of the loyal self as gathered here, would itself gather these hints for the developed doctrine which, with some omissions needed for popularization, directed his *Philosophy of Loyalty* in 1907.

5

Social
and
Political
Philosophy

We have explored Royce's 1888 development in metaphysics and morals. What remain to be investigated are his writings in social and political philosophy. Here a first reading may fascinate easily rather than inform accurately. Only gradually, through repeated thoughtful readings, does one discover that Royce's ideas in these areas are more carefully articulated and complex than one had at first suspected.

But the way in which Royce then dealt with sociopolitical questions deserves notice before we attempt to describe and evaluate his conclusions. He set as his aim "to become acquainted with the drift and the forces of Australasian life."[1] This intent breathed a healthy evolutionary positivism into his method. He resisted taking schemes from some a priori political science or sociology and reading Australia in their light. Rather, he searched empirically for the special factors at work in the evolving organization of the colonies' political and social life.[2] His sources included his personal on-the-

scene observations and the dialectic of contrary political
opinions such as Alfred Deakin and Sir Saul Samuel proposed to him. But his primary source was the experience and
reflection of others insofar as current Australian literature
brought these to his alert notice.[3] Besides official documents
and books on Australia, Royce found particular help in Australia's expertly edited, encyclopedic newspapers. Yet, despite continued readings, he frankly admitted that his own
writings on Australia were never more than mere opinions,
"stray impressions and reflections" by a wanderer.

Royce was convinced that the colonies' current social and
political life could not be well understood unless one grasped
how it had been shaped by geography, climate, and history.
By sketching these, he gave a sense of realism and evolution
to his initial account. In Australia's particularly monotonous,
weird, and even forbidding natural environment, a different
kind of frontiersman developed than in California: the
"Aussie," independent, self-reliant, and loyal, like the Australian backwoodsman who so fascinated Royce. The colonists' thinking was determined by the challenge, problem,
and hope of their frontier. For, except in the limited coastal
areas, Australia's agricultural growth depended upon re-
claiming semidesert lands or the desert itself.

Amazing patience and courage arose in a Wentworth, an
Oxley, a Stuart, and in other explorers of the colonies. Royce
felt that such sturdy souls "found an empire, and that too
even where they personally felt the most disappointment
with their discovery."[4] By their efforts they enriched others'
lives, even though they did not achieve their own purposes
and plans. In this way they exemplified what a later Royce
would call "giving oneself to a lost cause."

Thanks to the frontiersmen's persevering efforts, a set of
skills was gradually developed which made agriculture and

other industries possible. Colonists found grazing value in grasses once thought useless. They invented techniques to convert lands once thought barren into gardens and productive fields. Drought forced them gradually to recognize what treasure lay under their feet—springs, cave streams, and wells, even in the desert. By such arts Australia's high potential for agriculture and mining was harnessed. Royce summed up these accomplishments: "As a result of the war with the desert, and as an outcome of the wealth of successful stockraisers, farmers, and miners, we have at length the growing Australian civilization of today."[5]

On these foundations the Australians raised an elaborate social organization. It deeply impressed our American visitor —both in its political and in its nonpolitical forms.[6] Among the latter, he found it remarkably promising that in the colonies of Australia so many amateurs engaged so extensively in sports. He noted that this evoked a strong sense of community identification within clubs, groups, and colonies. Unlike our American hiring of professionals as our gladiators, the Australians had their groups' picked representatives. Thus, said Royce, "the people take warm interest, because it is the people who are carrying on the contest."[7]

If the "overtasked" professor, who had come to the South Seas for a cure, was impressed by the Australians' "love of healthy exercise and of sport," so, too, was he struck by their more relaxed pace of life which lacked "some of the elements of strain and worry that make our own [American] life bear so hard upon our constitutions. Competition is severe [in Australia] but not so merciless to the individual as with us."[8] Royce felt that the Australians would undergo more pressure as population grew and life's problems multiplied. Yet their enthusiasm for the outdoors and their trend to close social organization would safeguard them.

Another promising feature was the individual colonist's

loyalty to nonpolitical social institutions. Royce viewed this loyalty as the seed of success in such organizations. Unlike the "flippancy, irresponsibility, and rebelliousness" of the Californians of 1888, the colonists manifested "a degree of conservation, of public spirit, of social discipline, [and] of cheerful conformity to the general will of the community."[9] Royce implied that by accepting the importance of organized association, the loyal colonists, unlike many Americans, made a value judgment that was indispensable for maintaining a community.

During his forty years of teaching, Royce showed great reserve about publicly expressing his political philosophy.[10] That he broke this silence once with his Australian articles makes them especially significant. In "Reflections" he mentioned that the three topics of his political conversations with Deakin were: 1) the colonies' systems of responsible government, 2) the issue of colonial federation, and 3) the political future of Australasia.[11] These give us three dimensions of Royce's 1888 political thought. In all three he is distinctively concerned to locate the psychological conditions that render the relations between citizens fit or unfit. A similar interest controls his study of relations between citizens and their governmental ministers, or among these ministers themselves. Royce gave less attention to the colonists' imperial relationship to "Downing Street," except to note the colonists' growing independence of the crown. Though not marshaled together under his 1913 rubric of the "conditions required for the consciousness of community," Royce's 1888 emphasis on the psychological conditions for healthy political consciousness seems to foreshadow his later heuristic approach.[12]

Royce presented the facts, made contrasts with America, and evaluated. We follow his order. After a sketch of the colonies' geography and history, he focused on their current political situation. He was struck by how rapidly the colonies had developed their political organizations and how new some of their forms were. To his knowledge, these were the only pure democracies of British origin that now showed strongly socialist tendencies. For example, state ownership of the railways had existed from the start of the colonies. Royce asked what factors had tended to produce these habits of mind in people of English origin.[13] He noted, moreover, that the Australians' socialistic trend moved directly into economics and commerce. Among Americans, if socialist concern operated, it avoided government ownership of business, and moved along philanthropic lines of health, education, and welfare.

Royce more fully described Australian political life in his "Impressions."[14] Since the Australians frequently heard political speeches, they were continually agitated by state issues. Because their local government affairs seized their daily concern most strongly, the colonists focused narrowly on their own sparsely populated colony and felt an intense patriotism toward it. Furthermore, two factors usually speeded up the colonists' political machinery in its making and enforcing of laws. The people habitually and readily expressed their will. Then, too, their government ministers promptly translated the popular will into law because otherwise this same will might swiftly remove them from their untenured office.

The price of such mobility could be high at times. Being always on trial, the prime minister used up much time defending his party's actions before the colonial parliament. If his term had been fixed, as in American government, he could have better invested this time to design laws more accurately and to administer them more carefully. On the other hand, admittedly, he had less trouble from organized labor in the colonies that did his peer in America. For in Australia labor unions were committed to the general good rather than to a primary pursuit of their own interests. Hence, unlike American labor unions, they did not endanger the government. Fortunately, too, the Australians' nonpolitical organization was elaborate and thus worked as a mighty resistance against the trends toward precipitous lawmaking and demagoguery latent in the colonists' governmental systems.

But what historical factors chiefly contributed to develop such responsible governmental balance in these colonial systems? After a survey of the histories of New South Wales and Victoria, Royce pointed out that from the very beginning of these colonies, the government's position had been strong: "The organization of Crown colonies long preceded the coming of the mass of their population."[15] This led the colonists to expect strong governmental action if disorders arose. For example, when miners rioted at Ballarat in 1854, strong government forces imposed on them the will of organized society. By contrast, during the great riots in California's mining districts, miners feuded against rival miners, while a "deliberately incompetent political organization" lifted not a finger to stop them.[16] For the initial posture of Americans was one of suspicion toward government intervention. But in Australia, the colonists had a frank, intelligent confidence in the state's power for doing them much good. Reciprocally, governmental officials felt it their duty to answer the popular needs.

Royce emphasized that the government's initial position of strength reenforced the people in their esteem of the political order and evoked from them certain expectations and demands. Since they found their government backing up organized society against industrial forces disruptive of the economic whole, the people learned to accept active governmental entry into the business sector. Their basic perceptions of each other established their reciprocal roles. Thus the Australians saw their government primarily as a promoter of the economic order, whereas the Americans, sensing in government a possible interferer with free enterprise, adopted a defensive posture of "keep out." Royce's overall picture may serve to summarize: "Our early statesmen in this country used to fear nothing so much as the European tyrants who, no doubt, were longing to get at our liberties; hence our early tendency was mainly toward whatever secured popular freedom and checked the powers above. The Australian leader is nowadays thinking, it would seem, of nothing so much as of some new social tie by which he may persuade the popular will to bind itself. After all, are not social ties the glory of rational human life?"[17]

Besides strength, Royce pointed to "closeness" as a second cause in the colonists' development of a responsible political system. He put it clearly: "In Australia . . . the subject is always nearer to the State than he is with us, and that not merely because his State is a small province. Responsible ministerial government makes it always 'presidential year' with him, to use our own phrase. And the political eagerness of the people is not yet blunted, as with us, by the habitual cheapening of the issues of politics."[18] Numerically, psychologically, and morally the Australian was nearer to the state. Compared to the population of most American states, the small number of citizens in his own colony facilitated a sense of familiarity. Psychologically he was more involved because he felt more risk and power. Economics touched the colonist closely, yet few were more heavily involved in economics that his government. So when changes impended in governmental personnel or policies, the Australian experienced a heightened sense of risk. Accordingly he felt morally more obliged to regulate the government promptly and to face deep issues honestly, rather than to sidestep them for fear of stepping on the toes of vested interests.[19] Thus the Australians whom Royce interviewed actually found it hard to understand Americans' widespread lack of concern for their government's actions. In sum, Royce stressed that the different degrees of closeness between citizen and government make governments act differently.

Successful nonpolitical communities in Australia were built on loyalty, as we saw. But political organization—whether in the colonies, America, or elsewhere—is usually built on coercion.[20] Along with strength and closeness, then, coercion may be viewed as a third cause of the colonies' developing political systems. Royce pointed out a balance of coercions here. For those who possess state power, it is more expeditious to do things their own way, even if it means committing uncommitted majorities or pushing reluctant minorities. Meanwhile the Australian voters coerce their ministers by expecting to control both governmental policy-making and their ministers' duration in office. Because the voters' economic concern for governmental business activity is high, ministers feel forced to promise unfulfillable favors or to provide short-term placebos if they are to get elected or to stay in office. Here the Americans enjoyed a lesser degree of coercion, thanks to their reduced concern.

By these contrasts, Royce showed that the different communal consciousnesses of various peoples evoke different degrees of responsibility in governments. If one people frankly and confidently expects helpful services from its government, then an actively involved government emerges. But if another people jealously suspects the government of filching individual liberties and eagerly shows hostility against government intervention in economics, then a less active and less responsive ministry arises. Moreover, to the degree that both a people and its government ministers are more closely and tightly bound together in experiencing shared risks, to that degree do both become more responsible. By contrast, if citizens and officials are related more loosely, distantly, and apathetically to each other, they invite irresponsibility and tend to cheapen political issues.

Similarly, a people's expectations largely determine the qualities of its ministers. If Americans elect officials less qualified than an Alfred Deakin, then, suggested Royce, they get what they expect and deserve.[21] In the political cockpits of the colonies, a minister cannot last unless he is well trained in public affairs. He must be persistently resourceful and persuasive, as well as sensitive and plastic to the people's needs. Towards his many adroit rival politicians, he must exhibit tact rather than pugnaciousness. As "the good fencer," he must be a "graceful and pleasing artist," who leads the people and earnestly ministers to them. He must never descend to the role of a squabbling manager, or of an uncompromising prophet who stops the political process. He needs to balance his highly developed intelligence with his long practical training. Otherwise, he will either allow "abstract, vainly idealistic" theories to turn his head or permit the press of agenda to transform him into a mere bargainer. "In short," wrote Royce of government ministers, "they will be not only men of large ideas but men of business, . . . accustomed to feel the popular pulse, and conscious of the limitations of their practical life." Rather than fulminating and agitating rashly, as Sir Henry Parkes did when faced with the Chinese question in 1888, they will employ discretion concerning whether to speak, and if so, when and with what moderation and caution.[22] Royce, having surveyed the psychological conditions at work in the colonial political systems and in their government ministers, concluded with the wish that "our [American] public life were as certain to combine these important qualities in its ministers."

After this survey, Royce moved to evaluate the Australians' political systems. He found himself first raising some questions, then clarifying state socialism for himself, and finally focusing on two dangers and their remedies. The contrast between the Australians' involvement in government and the Americans' widespread apathy towards it raised one question that Royce left unsolved. What degree of risk and fear do citizens need to experience if they are to participate actively in government? When concluding the first installment of "Reflections," Royce sounded his second central and unsolved question.[23] How can a people hold the executive to that degree of responsibility which the needs of the people require, and yet grant him enough stability in office to escape the temptation of pushing drastic legislation through the assembly? Royce knew that to strike the balance wisely would benefit both Australian and American governments.

In the colonies he encountered a special kind of state socialism that prodded him to clarify his thinking with several significant distinctions. These reveal his efforts to sift through the altered conditions within the history of Australian colonial governments, and then to evaluate political systems accordingly. Thus he wrote: "An existing government, . . . a 'strong' government, found itself at first much embarrassed by the new-coming miners, undertook from the outset to regulate the use of the mines, was obliged to keep pace in its growth with the mainly economic needs of the country, and has so remained, ever since, the central object of social interest in the colonial mind."[24] In this way the correlative mentalities of the people and the government initiated and increased politically organized socialism in the colonies. With Royce, we can distinguish the mode of origin, the drift, and the level of Australian socialism.

First, state socialism may emerge naturally in accord with a people's genuine needs and temperament. But it can also be artificially imposed in accord with a design of a "Frankenstein sort."[25] Our American moves towards a protective tariff system and interstate commerce legislation were natural enough and, according to Royce, not even close to state social-ism.[26] Turning to the Australians' genuine state socialisms, however, he deeply suspected and dreaded that their types were too artificially designed "out of dead theories." They did not seem to him naturally faithful to emergent needs.

Secondly, the main concern or "drift" of socialistic think-ers in America and in Australia was different. As Royce described it: "Our [American] state socialists are generally philanthropists rather than men of business, and desire more to take care of the subject's soul and stomach than to carry his goods to market. But in the colonies the drift is the other way. The state is first in every man's thought, and its pur-poses are commercial rather than philanthropic."[27] The social thrust of the American government spent itself mainly in health, education, and welfare; it was heavily restricted from direct engagement in business. But the colonial governments were primarily economic and only philanthopic in a derivative way. With most Americans, Royce believed that state socialists of the "mainly economic" type could do "more serious mischief" than the "mainly philanthropic" breed.

Lastly, Royce distinguished state socialism as found at its theoretical and practical levels. Henry George's *Progress and Poverty* (1879) was an example of socialism at the abstract level. Royce regarded it as "shadowy," and thought of those who engage in socialist theories as "vainly idealistic" and even perhaps "mildly dangerous."[28] Quite different was Al-fred Deakin's practical art of socialistic governing. Deakin, in touch with the popular will and the interests of the various parties, was alert to current possibilities and their practical limits. He constantly tested whether certain steps were pre-mature or timely. Yet Royce had his reservations even with socialism taken simply as a practical art. Deakin's skills as a socialist minister puzzled Royce. He suspected that Deakin's methods of cabinet government were "too officious," that Deakin tended to fritter away time and energies in squabbles over trifles, and that he needed some brake—as yet undevised—against "quick drastic legislation."[29]

In sum, then, Royce distinguished six varieties of state socialism, according to origin, drift, and level. On none of them did he intend to render a final verdict. His examination of the Australians' experiments in socialism led him to clarify his thought on the topic and to adopt a more explicitly conservative stance towards socialism than he had evidenced before his voyage.[30] Royce confessed a fear of state socialism, even at the level of Deakin's practical art, because even there he saw the dangers of artificial design, officiousness, and potential demagoguery. The fear and suspicion he confessed in his Australian articles serve as a healthy corrective for those who fancy that totalitarian collectivism follows from Royce's later views of the loyal self and the Beloved Community. Those who so opine seem to have lost sight of the independence and self-reliance that are also integral to a Roycean loyal self.

In the colonies' political organization, our Australian visitor perceived two other dangers besides socialism. One was extravagant provincialism, in its various forms: political, economic, and cultural. Through the decades Royce was to wield his pen in fighting that beast. The other danger was an excessive activity and haste in forming political organizations. About the latter, he left only a few brief clues. But he poured out more than two thousand words to describe how "provincialism, . . . the great curse of the Australasian," takes various forms and grows. The remedies he suggested against it, however, seem more important: adopt wider ideals and take part in the ideals and the work of all peoples. This suggestion came in a long but telling quotation drafted more than fifty years before the United Nations' Declaration of Human

Rights. "The remedy for provincialism is of course always such a breadth of ideals and purposes as enables one, not to destroy, but to transcend, one's naturally narrow interests. Great nations are never without their provincial temperament, but they have become great by more or less completely humanizing their temperament, by sharing the ideals and the work of humanity without forgetting their private concerns."[31] This quotation instances the balance and complexity of Royce's thought. Yet, with its vague phrases, like "humanizing" and "sharing the ideals and the work of humanity," Royce's statement, however tantalizingly accurate, merely touches on themes that call for more articulate analysis. By often revisiting these themes in the remaining twenty-eight years of his life, he would work to clarify the ultimate sense of such phrases.

Most people would not recognize the burden of multiple responsibilities as a remedy for hasty and excessive political organization, the third danger which Royce foresaw for colonial government. Royce felt that a person with many duties would be more cautious about any impetuous move that would endanger several other responsibilities. At least against "Australia's other great evil, . . . overactivity and hasty organization in the political sphere," Royce recommended "such a wealth of political duties as forces a community to move deliberately and cautiously."[32] Very frequently a policy recommendation that looks bright enough in itself takes on a different hue when viewed through the complicated network of one's basic survival procedures already under way.

At the time of Royce's survey, there was a chief political duty that required cautious and deliberate movement by each colony. For, as Royce put it, "the chief hope of Australia must lie in the federation of her now disunited communities."[33] What was the present state of their federation question? Royce sketched how far the colonies' physical conditions and consciousness of this "cause" had evolved. Alongside hopeful happenings, he noticed South Australia's timidity towards federation and New South Wales's ridicule of it. Clearly the chief hope involved commercial as well as political negotiations. Royce also indicated two pseudocauses that hindered the colonists' pursuit of federation. First was the aforementioned extravagant provincialism in any of its forms. Also afloat, at the other extreme of opinion, was the romantic dream of forming one transcontinental "larger England" which was supposed to intensify the bonds of the present members of the British Empire by welding them all into one nation. Having already criticized extravagant provincialism, Royce now tested the viability of this greater imperial cause. With six pages of carefully reasoned arguments he seriously questioned its possibility.

As Royce discerned it, not imperial federation but colonial federation was the direction of the future. "The British Empire is already big with child, this child being the coming Australian nation. . . . Let the child be born, not prematurely, but in due time."[34] Australia's healthy development required such a separation of child from mother. The present need of the imperial connection for military and financial reasons was "great, but . . . not boundless." In time, with Australia's further growth, it would be much less needed.

Nor were reasons of affection moving in that direction, either. Royce pointed out four signs of a "growing spirit of independence in the colonies"—countersigns to the "mere sentiment of imperial loyalty."

First of all, the crown's recent attempt to appoint a governor of Queensland had caused much trouble because the crown had not consulted in advance with Queensland whether the proposed candidate was acceptable. Second, as a general rule now, the colonies were unwilling to submit to the "Downing Street" influence on home and foreign policies. Furthermore, beneath the colonists' passionate anti-Chinese agitation in May and June 1888, one pervasive consensus was felt: If Australian interests conflicted with imperial policy, then, "the imperial policy must simply give way." And finally, the young Australian party, that vigorously growing seed of Australia's future, favored eventual independence of an Australian nation.

Interestingly, the way in which Royce argued this political question was not by deduction from moral principles, but rather by induction towards "the actual tendency of social evolution in Australia." The basis offered for so arguing sounds about as naturalistic as can be imagined in an "idealist" like Royce: "Social duties never run utterly counter to social facts, but depend upon a sound and just use of the facts."[35] Here we find yet another instance of Royce's empiricism.

Royce next peered beyond the eventual federation of the colonies. He broadened his scope to include Australia, New Zealand, Oceania, and the East Indies, along with China, India, and Russia. Amid such a startlingly new context and its much mistier possibilities, he inquired what roles these embryonic nations of Australasia would play in world civilization. Royce knew the importance of discerning at long range the leading political roles that New Zealand and Australia would be called upon to play in Australasia. He was sensitive to the powerful positions of Australasia's neighbors, China, India, and Russia—even if he did not mention Japan explicitly.[36] In his eyes, the threatened immigration of Chinese into Australia—a threat that occasioned the 1888 disturbance in Sydney—was simply symptomatic of a relationship that had to be worked out. He concluded that this "Chinese Question" would largely occasion the separation of Australia from the British Empire. Though this prediction proved erroneous, his argument leading to it seems significant for current political philosophy.

In brief, Royce argued that he had found in basic racial homogeneity a limiting condition for the political life of a great nation. Attempts to build a nation out of different races incurred "endless possible complications" and "inevitable disagreements." If force was applied to the racial minority and the attendant evils arose, there was, at the very least, the risk of fracturing the basic national consensus. Or there was the risk of losing plurality-consensus, the basis for that political unity which a great nation requires. I leave to the reader to discern whether in the following passage Royce displayed a hard-nosed realism, or an anglophile sense of superiority, or a waspish white racism, or something else. Turning to our American attempt to build a great nation with a black minority, he made a dire prediction that nearly a century of history has not falsified: "[Here is] something far more significant than a hatred of cheap labor, or even a contempt for an alien race. We in this country have suffered and will yet suffer far too deeply from the presence in our midst of a few million very docile and well-meaning negroes to be in a position to doubt the dangers of founding a great nation, in a new country, upon the basis of race heterogeneity." For Royce there is great danger even in mixing different strains of the very same race: "Even the mixture of the European stocks themselves, although it is inevitable, involves as here in America, evils enough on the way." But to go further and mix the races themselves would certainly spell greater evils.

Accordingly, when founding their new nation, the Australians would be "hanging the millstone round their own necks" if they granted the Chinese such free access as would allow them to grow within fifty years to a quarter of Australia's population. Royce conceded that to forestall such an influx of Chinese the Australians would have to assume towards China "an attitude that must at best be frequently unfriendly," but one that in the end would be "the highest political wisdom." The price of becoming a great nation was politically to limit one's welcomes and maintain control of one's admissions. "We did not create the Orientals," wrote Royce, ". . . but we are to blame if, knowing the inevitable disagreements that must result, we invite them to help us form a great nation in our own territory." Such realistic limits cause one to doubt a primarily romantic reading of Royce's later philosophy of the Beloved Community.

In the Roycean thesis of 1888, "Race homogeneity is the basis of healthy national life," it is unfortunately implied that healthy national life, or a great nation, only occurs with white race homogeneity—and preferably Anglo-Saxon race homogeneity. Royce's pronounced bias that white Anglo-Saxon culture was, overall, ultimately superior to all other cultures was widespread in his era. Like many of his contemporaries, Royce was caught in a monocultural pattern and feared the loss of Anglo-Saxon cultural dominance in the immigrant tide of Latins, Semites, and Slavs.[37]

Having found in one popular writing of Royce's early period a preference for white dominance, we need to view it in the context of his long-term, personal concern to promote interracial justice and to reduce racial prejudice. For instance, later on he often delivered a lecture examining racial antipathies and illusions. In 1913 he developed his doctrine that the heart of genuine loyalty must pulse with the will to do atoning deeds that reconcile alienated human beings.[38] Moreover, even while dissenting from Royce's 1888 preference for white dominance, one can concede him a certain perspicacity.[39] For Royce saw acutely that race operates at a level far deeper than skin pigmentation and creates profound differences. This led him to face the polar tension between one's loyalties to all mankind and to his own race. Practically Royce solved it by favoring that particular loyalty which possessed the better organizations for fulfilling specific duties. Comparing a person's dual responsibility to mankind and to his country (preferably homogeneous in race), Royce stated: ". . . however loyal we try to be to humanity, we cannot forget that such loyalty must for many centuries to come be expressed only in concrete, and therefore in somewhat exclusive, national organizations."[40] Admittedly, multinational corporations, mass media, and the United Nations supply us with a viewpoint very different from Royce's. Yet even in 1888, he advocated loyal dedication to further the moral insight in any man and to support responsible development in education everywhere. Hence, in the text above, his requirement of "many centuries" seems a pretension, and his exclusive "only" surprises many by its lack of qualification.

Royce returned to this polar tension between one's country and mankind in his 1891 article: "Human brotherhood is a noble thing; but political unity is a matter of stern justice as well as of home-seeking devotion. You best honor both the justice and the devotion when you confine their work within easily intelligible boundaries."[41] By opposing what is noble and what is stern justice, Royce invited his reader to think that strict justice operates only in a political unity with its positive law obligations, and not between men of different countries simply *qua* men. By preferring that one confine himself within easily intelligible boundaries, such as civil law responsibilities, Royce downplayed the more basic values and duties of human beings *qua* human. Such values and correlative duties are too vital to be boxed within easily intelligible boundaries; rather, they are exempt from boundaries of nation and race, because deeper than either. Royce seems here to have given undue emphasis to specifiable values and in this way to have blocked himself from an inclusive pursuit of all the basic human values wherever man is found and to whatever race he belongs. These fundamental values would certainly include every individual human life, every promotion of moral insight, every fostering of that respect and concern which bond people humanly.

We extend our evaluation beyond Royce's view of the tension between mankind and its nations (and races) to Royce's 1888 social and political thought generally. What were its strengths and shortcomings? We begin with some strengths. Royce operated with a clear distinction between community and society, even if he did not use those terms as technically as Tönnies was later to use *Gemeinschaft* and *Gesellschaft*. For Royce a people was more basic and significant than a state. So, rather than employing government, he was inclined to rely mainly on nonpolitical forces such as race, commerce, culture, and religion to secure and promote a people's healthy unity. His recognition that greater power for building world community lies in nonpolitical fields would increasingly come into play as Royce entered his final years.[42] Our experience of the organizations auxiliary to the United Nations would confirm this view.

Secondly, Royce showed how the variable psychic stances of citizens and officials, ranging from apathy to close involvement, determine the quality of political life in a state. His concern to uncover the five conditions for the shared consciousness distinctive of a genuine community became explicit only in his 1913 classic, *The Problem of Christianity*.[43] Yet already in his 1888-1891 writings, he tried to lay bare the conscious conditions—attitudes, expectations, felt risks, and so forth—that made the political consciousness of Australians different from that of Americans. Moving to social life generally—in its nonpolitical as well as political forms—Royce investigated how even apparently trivial details significantly alter a group's social consciousness. He also studied how the Australians' more widespread commitment to engage in amateur sports and to live outdoors differentiated them from Americans. He asked the basic question, How did the Australians' greater respect for social order and organizations open up new possibilities of communal life which customary American rebelliousness and alienation forestalled? Here he seems to have pioneered in advance of George Herbert Mead, who was Royce's pupil in the fall of 1887, and also in advance of James Baldwin, who was a coresearcher with Royce in social psychology during the nineties.

Thirdly, Royce's complex mind was convinced that keeping in realistic touch with social consciousness requires a practical balancing of many polarities. For him, social life consisted in interactions that needed a balanced "give and take" between citizens and officials, among the several colonies, and between each colony and the crown or Asiatic power. Although we just expressed our reservations about one dimension of Royce's polarities-in-balance, nevertheless, Royce's cultivated sensitivity to the overall need of balancing reciprocal relations deserves commendation. In his Australian articles, we found him concerned to harmonize various polarities—of the self and mankind, of a small state and a political "federation of mankind," of "home-seeking devotion" and universality of intent, of self-reliance and loyalty. For example, he did not allow the grand ideal of universal community to lift his feet off the ground, but pragmatically required some businesslike art of patiently working here and now through extant practicable forms towards a somewhat better realization of that ideal in the near future. In his basic intellectual life-style, Royce was convinced that any approach to wisdom required, beyond all the needed analyses, a synthetic effort of balanced opposites, done with as much rigor and criticality as one could muster. This gives us a glimpse into Royce's complex mind.

A man's shortcomings are often the unconscious deposits of his own limited cultural environment. Such were Royce's 1888 shortcomings. Contrasted against his mental depth and breadth in 1916, they reveal what a surprising purification was at work in this mind which was so early dedicated to a critical quest for more truth.

Here we merely touch upon a Westerner's prejudice and his notion of a human right. In his Australian writings, Royce exhibited a commonly held Western prejudice that, because of destiny or historical necessity, "Europe will of course in time master by far the larger part of both Asia and Africa."[44] To say that Western technology, science, and urbanization tend to so dominate is hardly the same as to declare that Western life-styles, ideas, political power, and economics will surely so dominate. Much less is it to say that Western colonization and empire building will "of course" master Asia and Africa, as Royce opined.

His sense of white superiority led him to another unfortunate expression: "Australia, when she grows a great nation, is to be the first civilized power of the Pacific, and as such must always steadily strive to restrain the influence of China . . . since Australia must be distinctly . . . opposed to the Chinese Empire in the Pacific."[45] Even if we recall that Royce may here have viewed China and Japan in Asia rather than in the Pacific, we still can hardly save this statement. For he does not refer to them as venerable civilizations. Nor does he suggest that the Australians might enrich their culture by studying Oriental ideas—at least as a counterbalance to Anglo-American ideas. Rather, his articles create the impression that to be Europeanized is to be civilized, but to be Oriental is to be barbarian. Furthermore, by emphasizing the need to restrain the "Chinese Empire in the Pacific," he assumed that the much more foreign British Empire was far more clearly entitled to rule in the Pacific with ever growing influence.

We would not ordinarily expect such an 1888 anglophile to become a pioneer in initiating dialogue between philosophies of the East and West. But fortunately, Royce so developed. Nor would we look for the man who penned such myopic lines to become "ecumenical" among world religions. Yet Royce grew sufficiently in mental stature to draft an instructive comparison of Buddhism and Christianity, and a masterpiece in the philosophy of religion.[46] Like most of us, Royce tended to identify his historical accidents with what is right. He was proud of having English blood, California independence, and a Harvard position. Like us, he subconsciously felt that blood, birthplace, and career other than one's own were somehow not quite as good as one's own.

Secondly, Royce showed a strength and a weakness in his notion of a human right. On the one hand, as he considered the traditional Anglo-American notion of a human right, he caught the exaggeration of its primarily defensive stance—a stance which our American overeagerness for rebellion and pure self-reliance stiffened. So, as a counterpoise, he reached out appreciatively to the Australian's greater respect for the social order. But, on the other hand, the Royce of 1888 was simply not yet aware of the inherent ontological dignity within personal being. As a result, he was not yet able to root his notion of human right in the central grounding fact that the human person is as essentially social as he is essentially individual and unique.[47]

In any overall evaluation, however, one needs to emphasize that Royce's 1888 growth in metaphysics, ethics, and social and political philosophy far outdistanced the negative factors just mentioned. In October 1888 that acute observer of men, William James, reported, "Royce is back from his voyage round the world, as fresh as a new-born babe, and as full of promise."[48] This perceptive psychologist spied in Royce's mind a new vitality, balance, and verve that enabled Royce characteristically to achieve that "freer simple touch with deepest relations"—to employ James's later description of Royce's distinctive philosophical acumen.[49]

6

Philosophical Links with the Early Nineties

We have advanced an interpretation of Royce's metaphysical, ethical, and sociopolitical thought in 1888. Can we test our interpretation? Does it fit in closely with what Royce revealed of his philosophical positions shortly after he returned to America—specifically, with his expressions of the early nineties? Circumstances compel us to limit our test of basic correspondence to his metaphysics and ethics. For astonishingly, after his Australian writings Royce did not offer any similarly clear and extensive expression of his sociopolitical views.

By which criteria, then, shall we measure his 1888 metaphysics and ethics against those of the early nineties? We select Royce's "insight through Schroeder" of about 1891 and ask whether it is continuous with his concern with the "self" which deepened in Australia. We also choose his first major philosophical writings after his return: the popular synthesis of his metaphysics in his 1892 *Spirit of Modern Philosophy,* and his more technical 1892 article, "The Implications of Self-Consciousness."[1]

After his return from the South Seas and after 1890, but many years before his 1899 Gifford Lectures, Royce experienced a moderate philosophical breakthrough. For he reported being "much struck by the remarkable proof, in the first volume [1890] of [Ernst] Schroeder's *Algebra der Logik.*"[2] The proof showed that if one provisionally regards as the "whole of the universe" any simply defined universe of classes of objects, *and* if one simply reflects on these classes from a new viewpoint, then contradictions arise since the new secondary realm lies outside the "whole of the universe." Following this clue, Royce penetrated to the metaphysical significance of Schroeder's proof; namely, that no one can come to any ultimate human definition of the genuine whole of the universe unless he comes round in the end to employing an endless process of self-reflection. Royce's own words surpass any attempt at paraphrase: "The true totality of Being can therefore only be defined by an endless process, or is an endless reflective system. This proof of Schroeder's first brought home to me the fact that the necessity for defining reality in self-reflecting or endless terms is not dependent upon any one metaphysical interpretation of the world, whether realistic or idealistic, but is the consequence of a purely abstract account of the formal Logic of the concept of Reality in any of its forms."[3] The concept of Reality, however interpreted, necessarily requires that an endless self-reflective process be the basic structure of any true definition of Reality as a whole. Central here is a reflection, by a self, of a self. Such self-reflection inevitably includes an endless series of other finite selves within an actually Infinite Self. By 1899, Royce came to regard "this result as of the greatest weight for any metaphysical enterprise." For he had discovered that "this truth is common property for all, whether realists or idealists, whether sceptics or dogmatists." Hence, around 1891 Royce had, in one key sense, already delved "beyond idealism and realism." For he had penetrated to a self-reinstating, and thus undeniable, structure present in any meaning of Reality as a whole, whether conceived by dogmatist or sceptic, realist or idealist. Consequently, Royce's insight through Schroeder would be highly significant for the middle and final stages of his philosophy.

But is it clearly linked with his Australian sojourn? A suggestion from Royce points to an affirmative answer. In 1899, as he reviewed his intellectual development since 1885, Royce reported that during this period he had not changed his definition of truth but shifted his interest to clarify "the special problems of human life and destiny."[4] In 1885, he had "not emphasized prominently enough" will and experience in the Absolute. Hence, he continued, "the aspects of the Absolute Life which they [will and experience] denote have since [1885] become more central to my own interests." So Royce saw himself from 1885 to 1899 as making will and experience more central in his philosophy. He came to focus less exclusively on thought and more inclusively on life and purpose, deliberately synthesizing all life's meanings through interrelating individuals. Now what role did his insights of 1888 and about 1891 play in this overall development?

As we saw, Royce's Australian experience of 1888 provided him with a deepened taste for life and for the loyal self's free pursuit of ideals. On this cruise, he chose to keep putting first priority on true knowing rather than to follow Martineau and to place it on action. Yet maintaining this first priority did not keep Royce from roaming where the "fields of speculation are very wide and romantic" in search of life's many meanings, particularly "about Freedom and the Ideals."[5] As we saw, his explosive "metaphysical speculation" had prompt repercussions in his ethical, social, and political thought.

Accordingly, we may summarize Royce's overall philosophic growth in 1888 as follows: It disposed Royce to focus on any dynamic of life and its meaning not only in such contexts as intellectual judgments and formal logic, but also and increasingly, in affective experiences, voluntary choices, and ego-alter relationships. This is the main conclusion of our investigation. To put it conservatively, then, Royce's deeper appreciation of concrete life and individuals, which he gained in Australia, was at least one operative ingredient which thereafter moved him, in his post-1888 metaphysics, to put more prominent emphasis on will and experience, on self and individual, amid his earlier categories of thought and Logos. On his return, then, with his consciousness heightened to attend to the self and to its free self-reflection, Royce would have been particularly sensitive around 1891 to catch the metaphysical import of Schroeder's remark. In this way his Australian experience seems a quite probable ground for Royce's insight through Schroeder. Moreover, the latter seems to be a coherent growth from his 1888 "metaphysical speculation."

To submit our interpretation to another test, we turn to our second norm, a pair of Royce's 1892 writings. In *The Spirit of Modern Philosophy*, he popularly summarized his central position, and in his "Implications" article he brought this summary to more technical expression.[6] "Implications" is an especially fitting norm for measuring the new game he had bagged in 1888. For following the journey it is his first technical attempt at rigorous expression of what he called his "ethical interpretation of reality." In it we find Royce carrying to the academic public what he had promised to share with James.[7]

In general, both "Implications" and his popular summary reveal his new sense of life, awakened in Australia. Both speak in Royce's new categories of self, person, reflective self-consciousness and, at least in "Implications," of the individual.[8] Both are much concerned with the "old trouble about Continuity" and the "question about Freedom and the Ideals." In both writings, the Australian speculation which led Royce to distinguish between appreciation and description continues to insert that distinction and to produce its effects.[9]

Most significantly, however, the ethically just viewpoint emerges as an essential ingredient for constituting the self-reflective individual and his life. If the self lacks this viewpoint, there is an essential inadequacy in its grasp of the difference between a true meaning and an erroneous meaning. By 1892, Royce's ethical norm has become "a Self that can reflect with justice and clearness."[10] Royce's evident growth in understanding loyalty during 1888 has now led logically and historically to his "ethical interpretation of reality" in his 1892 writings. These latter specify both appreciation of and commitment to moral value as requisites for an essentially complete self-reflective process.

If we further compare his Australian writings with his "Implications" article and with the popular summary, we find three additional points of basic similarity. First, Royce continued his theme of the immanence of the Infinite within the finite while rejecting either a dichotomy between or a confusion of the two. In 1892 he wrote: "The finite does not vanish in him ["the Infinite . . . Person"]; but he [the Infinite] appears to us, although very imperfectly, through and by means of the finite."[11] Secondly, the questions of self-identity and self-identifiability were as central in 1892 as they were in Royce's marginalia on Martineau aboard the *Freeman*.[12] Finally, at the close of "Implications," the philosopher sketched the fully developed human self. In this sketch,

Royce uses his ethical viewpoint to unite the self's historically embodied actions (sociopolitical thought) with the self's free willing to know personally the eternally True (metaphysics). In 1888 he had promised to share with James how "I have largely straightened out the big metaphysical tangle about continuity, freedom, and the world-formula, which, as you remember, I had aboard with me when I started."[13] Now he lets others share in his insight: "Every being who is rationally conscious of time, is, by that very fact, living in part out of the world of time. For what we know we transcend. To live in time by virtue of one's physical nature, but out of time by virtue of one's very consciousness of time itself, is to share in the eternal freedom, and to be a moral agent."[14]

In these ways, then, our two criteria confirm the interpretation that Royce's intellectual development in 1888 was significantly large and strategically important for his future philosophic maturity.

7

Epilogue:
Journey
Home

After his stay in Australia, Royce invested a month lingering in New Zealand. He visited Auckland, Wellington, and the volcanic regions of the North Island. As previously noted, he found New Zealand's climate even more restorative than Australia's, and the Maoris were especially fascinating to him. Having completed what he called his "stay in paradise," Royce boarded the steamer *Alameda*, under the command of Master H. G. Morse. In three weeks he crossed the Pacific and on August 3 arrived within the Golden Gate.[1]

Enjoying excellent health as he stepped ashore in his native California, Royce quickly encountered some of the bitterness of life. Six weeks earlier his pioneer father, the senior Josiah Royce, worn out by years of toiling in a broken body, had died in Los Gatos. At that time Royce's mother, Sarah Eleanor, had been away in nearby San Jose nursing a gravely sick daughter, Ruth, who had not entirely recovered even by the time her distinguished brother arrived for a family visit in early August. At Los Gatos Royce found both his mother and

Ruth grief-stricken.[2] Here Josiah felt his powerlessness. He had been away when his family needed him most. Now when present he was unable to provide much financial help during their need. So he deeply felt how the previous carelessness with his own health had hurt others too. To William James he confided: "Help from a good son who had been careful of his health and of his means wouldn't be a bad thing. . . . But I won't let myself be discouraged. The devil has had his own in my past. Perhaps he won't have so much in my future. We shall see."[3] During these weeks Royce probably accompanied Sarah Eleanor on a visit to Oak Hill cemetery in San Jose to visit his father's grave. If so, his father's memory could hardly have failed to activate this young Josiah's "cult of the dead," and to promote his rededication to philosophical pioneering.

After some weeks with the bereaved, Royce returned to Harvard. As a fitting finale to his round-the-world trip, his train sped him past beautiful Mount Shasta and then through the majestic Canadian Rockies in all their multifaceted splendor. Yet the mountains were only an external symbol of that interior multifaceted splendor we have here found in Royce—the correspondent, patient, naturelover, and adventurer; the metaphysician, ethician, and student of society and politics.

Happy to be back home again with his wife Katharine and their boys, Royce wrote to his mentor, Daniel Coit Gilman, "I feel like a bent bow, all ready to twang."[4]

If the reader has seen that the present work is integrated around the idea of community which, in turn, has the idea of loyalty at its center, then he has recognized the order of this study. For the first part explored the affective and volitional side of Royce's personality. This background was needed to understand Royce the man who philosophizes.

The second part of the study, the principal investigation, entered directly into Royce's intellectual life and found his "metaphysical speculation" leading Royce through the World of Description into the World of Appreciation. Thus Royce won the ground for his doctrine of community. Then, through analysis of Royce's marginalia on Martineau, we confirmed this insight and manifested Royce's ultimate basis for community and loyalty in the all-knowing and all-appreciative One. However, by permitting moral evil, this Infinite Self seemed disloyal to his own universe; he apparently excluded even the possibility of such freedom and knowledge as are required by loyalty among human selves and by loyalty between them and God. Royce responded by clarifying the relation between moral values and this Infinite Self. The latter was recognized as the One who affirmatively initiates, appreciates, restores, and governs community through moral values even though the ignorant and alienating finite selves, by their free decisions, sometimes stray from loyal realization of moral values.

Next, when the study surveyed a dozen ingredients in Roycean loyalty, it was actually exploring the structures of genuine community consciousness. This study of loyalty became concrete in Royce's description of the Australian backwoodsman.

Then for the first and last time in his life Royce provided an overall sketch of his social and political philosophy. This not only illustrated his embodiment of loyalty in concrete social and political conditions, but also called attention to some important restrictions needed when scholars interpret Royce's philosophy of loyalty.

The third part of the study tested the validity of the findings of this investigation. It asked whether Royce's subsequent writings manifested the presence of the new insights and doctrines reportedly gained during the 1888 experience, and thus it checked these against evidences Royce offered in his writings completed between 1888 and 1892.

From this outline the reader may now recognize more starkly Royce's 1888 philosophical method as it operates within the baselines of four major doctrines and typically advances through four procedural steps.

Doctrinally, Royce chooses to believe that appreciative knowing brings a knower to a deeper level of reality than does descriptive knowing. In other words, Royce holds that intersubjective knowledge of the ego-alter type is more concrete, vital, and interpersonally significant than is the indispensable, powerful, but abstract way of knowing that characterizes the positive sciences. Secondly, the intersubjective community entered by appreciative knowing can be morally sound only if genuine loyalty animates its members and thus orients them to all mankind without exclusion. Thirdly, by recognizing that true appreciative knowing of being-in-community is more fundamental than human feeling, freedom, and activity, Royce establishes his basic metaphysical order, in contrast to that of James Martineau whom he criticizes. Finally, Royce grounds these three doctrinal options in the taproot of his thought, the idea of the all-knowing and all-loving Other as the ultimate explanation of reality. Thus he retains and enriches his fundamental "religious insight" of 1883.

A quartet of procedural choices also marks Royce's 1888 method. His philosophy first penetrates through scientific knowledge (the World of Description) to that lived union with other beings with minds (the World of Appreciation). Vitally present to other selves, Royce next forms an appreciative understanding of them. Then moving into a procedure of contrast-comparison, Royce finds or invents a "third idea" which accurately accounts for the differences between the selves or their psychic products and which then reconciles and mediates them into some vital union. Since this "third idea" occurs within Royce's fundamental commitment to promote the genuine life of loyalty everywhere (and thus to advance the universal community), it must in the end call for practical action of some constructive kind.

These four procedural steps in Royce's method can be discerned in this study when Royce reflects philosophically. For example, when he, then thirty-two years old, sits on the deck of the Australia-bound *Freeman* and ponders the pages of James Martineau's *A Study of Religion,* he first gets in living touch with Martineau's mind through this book, then gradually fashions his own interpretation of Martineau's meaning, then finds or invents some "third idea" as a basis for agreeing or disagreeing with Martineau, and finally, under Martineau's overall influence, is led in practice to regard God less exclusively as the Knower and more as the Infinite Other Self whose appeal, experience, and will is present to Royce and all finite selves. Of course, such a "minor" revision of Royce's idea of God would have momentous practical consequences.

In conclusion, the reader is invited to test further the claims of the present study by measuring the consistency of the insights here highlighted with the Roycean writings of 1892-1916 and with the investigations of Roycean scholars.

Notes

Preface

1. See the "Autobiographical Sketch," in Royce's *The Hope of the Great Community* (New York: Macmillan, 1916), pp. 122-23 (hereafter *HGC*).

2. See Royce's "Last Lectures in Metaphysics, Notes of Lectures delivered by Josiah Royce in Phil. 9, Metaphysics, 1915-1916," lecture of January 11, 1916, p. 130, Richard C. Cabot Papers, Harvard Archives, Cambridge, Mass. (quoted with permission; hereafter LLM).

3. Date inferred from LLM, p. 135. Royce soon published this insight in chaps. 11 and 12 of his first major work, *The Religious Aspect of Philosophy* (Boston: Houghton Mifflin, 1885), pp. 384-474 (hereafter *RAP*).

4. In *The World and the Individual*, 2 vols. (New York: Macmillan, 1899, 1901), 2:vii (hereafter *WI*), Royce publicly acknowledged having abandoned his former scepticism.

5. LLM, lecture of January 11, 1916, p. 130.

6. For a fuller description and supporting texts, see Frank Oppenheim, "Josiah Royce's Intellectual Development: An Hypothesis," *Idealistic Studies* 6 (January 1976): 85-102.

7. See LLM, p. 130, and *WI*, 2:vii.

8. See LLM, pp. 134-35, for this and the next quotation.

9. Ibid., p. 134. In this recollection of how he was led to his argument drawn from the possibility of error, Royce mentioned explicitly that one of the motives was the responsibility he felt to provide sound guidance to his students.

10. See *WI*, 1:553, n. 1.

11. For Royce's acknowledgments of Bradley's influence on him, see Royce's *The Conception of God*, 2d ed. (New York: Macmillan, 1897), p.

141, n. 1 (hereafter *CG*), and *WI*, 1:474. For some years after the 1893 publication of Bradley's *Appearance and Reality*, Royce employed it as a textbook in his metaphysics course.

12. Hints of this interaction between Royce and G. H. Howison appear in the 1897 edition of *CG*. For example, see Howison's essay (pp. 81-132), Royce's acknowledgment (pp. 136-37), and then the editorial notes that Howison appended to Royce's "Supplementary Essay," (pp. 181, 321, 332, and 333). But for the even more revealing Royce-Howison correspondence, see Royce to Howison, August 31, 1896, in *The Letters of Josiah Royce*, ed. John Clendenning (Chicago: University of Chicago Press, 1970), pp. 347-48.

13. Royce to G. H. Howison, August 31, 1896, *Letters*, p. 347.

14. Royce to James, June 21, 1901, *Letters*, p. 422. Recognizing the major impact these Piercean lectures had on his intellectual development, Royce wrote, not the expected "epoch-making," which is implied, but "epoch-marking," which provides an instance of Royce's retrospective interpretation of an event's significance for his own thought growth.

15. Royce to Mary Whiton Calkins, March 20, 1916, *Letters*, p. 645. See also LLM, pp. 130 and 135.

16. Royce to Mary Whiton Calkins, March 20, 1916, *Letters*, p. 645.

17. See Royce's "First Berkeley Lecture, 1914," vol. 84, no. 3, pp. 5-14, Royce Papers, Harvard Archives (quoted with permission). The central texts comprising this Roycean confession have been published in Oppenheim, "Hypothesis," pp. 85-86 and 99.

18. See his *The Philosophy of Loyalty* (New York: Macmillan, 1908), pp. viii, 9, 56, and 197 (hereafter *PL*).

19. See John Clendenning's "Introduction" in *Letters*, pp. 9-40, and Oppenheim's "Hypothesis." Moreover, even though Bruce Kuklick's full-length study, *Josiah Royce: An Intellectual Biography* (Indianapolis, Ind.: Bobbs-Merrill, 1972), assigns exclusive primacy to logic in Royce's thought growth, this recent work contributes significantly to research on Royce.

20. Each year two studies of Royce's biography and intellectual development—by John Clendenning from the perspective of American studies and by Frank Oppenheim from the perspective of philosophical issues—are moving nearer to publication.

21. During this voyage Royce experienced an appeal-and-response dynamism operating between the egos and alter egos he encountered in various political and nonpolitical communities, as well as between the finite human ego and the Infinite Alter Ego mediated by the human community. Such experience provided an empirical basis for his insight into loyalty.

22. Of the new life a recuperating Royce experienced after his long period of depression, he wrote, "now that passion has come again, and the good Lord seems to have some life in his world . . ." (*Letters*, p. 215).

23. See *HGC*, p. 129.

24. See *RAP*, pp. 384-474, esp. pp. 424-25.

25. See *Fugitive Essays by Josiah Royce*, ed. J. Loewenburg (Cambridge, Mass.: Harvard University Press, 1920), p. 7 (hereafter *FE*).

26. In Josiah Royce, *The Problem of Christianity*, 2 vols. (New York: Macmillan, 1913), lectures 11 and 12, 2: 109-221 (hereafter *PC*); cf. Oppenheim, "Hypothesis," pp. 85-86 and 98-101).

27. Royce to James, May 21, 1888, *Letters*, p. 216.

1

1. James to Santayana, April 22, 1888, William James Papers, Houghton Library, Harvard University, Cambridge, Mass.

2. The principal sources of the present study include: Royce's letters to Francis Ellingwood Abbot, Alfred Deakin, Daniel Coit Gilman, William James, Charles Rockwell Lanman, Horace Elisha Scudder—especially during this period of spring and summer, 1888; Royce's 1888 marginalia in James Martineau's *A Study of Religion*, 2 vols. (Oxford: Clarendon, 1888), as reserved in the Robbins Library, Harvard; Royce's two published articles describing his Australasian experiences: "Reflections after a Wandering Life in Australasia," *Atlantic Monthly* 63 (1889): 675-86, and 813-28; "Impressions of Australia," *Scribners Magazine* 9 (1891): 75-87; C. R. Lanman's diary for this period; the *Los Gatos* (Cal.) *News*, Aug. 23-24, 1888; J. A. La Nauze, *Alfred Deakin*, 2 vols. (Cambridge, England: Cambridge University Press, 1965); Walter Murdoch, *Alfred Deakin: A Sketch* (London: Constable & Co., 1923). Most of this correspondence is now available in *The Letters of Josiah Royce*, ed. John Clendenning (Chicago: University of Chicago Press, 1970), esp. pp. 211-26, or in Ralph Barton Perry's *The Thought and Character of William James*, 2 vols. (Boston: Little, Brown, & Co., 1935), vol. 1 (hereafter *TCWJ*), or in the works of La Nauze and Murdoch.

3. See Oppenheim, "Hypothesis," pp. 89, 95-99.

4. See Royce to James, May 21, 1888, *Letters*, p. 216.

5. Ibid.; "Universal Thought" refers to the terminus of Royce's theistic argument in *RAP*, chap. 11, esp. pp. 423-35.

6. James to Royce, August 24, 1888, *TCWJ*, 1:802.

7. *Letters*, p. 211.

8. Milton R. Konvitz, review of *The Basic Writings of Josiah Royce,* ed. John J. McDermott (Chicago: University of Chicago Press, 1969), in *Saturday Review,* Jan. 24, 1970, p. 29.

9. Josiah Royce, *The Spirit of Modern Philosophy* (Boston: Houghton Mifflin, 1892), pp. 342-44 (hereafter *SMP*). Royce and William James concurred that in general one's temperament determines one's philosophy. But unlike James, Royce specified that one's "essential temperament" is what truly determines one's philosophy and that only by a careful study of the history of philosophy can one learn which ideals have permanent human value and thus discover the difference between one's accidental and essential temperament.

10. Royce referred at least twice to the manuscript he mailed to his wife from Melbourne at no small expense; see *Letters,* pp. 213 and 215. This story of his outbound voyage, most likely in the form of a journal, is not extant in Roycean deposits known to the present writer. If found, it would critically control much of the present study.

11. Some may wish a closer look at these objections and the evidence behind the terse replies in the text. A first objection: was not Royce's 1888 round-the-world voyage a pleasantly restful cruise designed mainly to cure an "over-tasked man" (*Letters,* p. 214) and thus a very unlikely situation for any significant intellectual growth? The objection overlooks the recorded phenomenon that great minds fairly often find insights dawning when they move towards, or live within, the leisure that follows intense toil and fruitless search for an answer. (This theme recurs in Rollo May's *The Courage to Create* [New York: W. W. Norton, 1975] and is underscored by B. F. J. Lonergan in his *Insight* [New York: Philosophical Library, 1957], chap. 1.) One recalls Archimedes' "Eureka!" while he relaxed in the baths of Syracuse, after his long unsuccessful search to find a way to test the purity of the gold in the king's crown. We know Royce had long struggled with a "big metaphysical tangle" before sailing. What more likely occasion for an intellectual breakthrough than when, recuperated and relaxed, he rested "amid the trade-winds, and under the softly flapping canvas" (*Letters,* p. 217)?

A second objection: when writing to William James, did not Royce confess, "In the deepest of my nothingness I read . . . Martineau . . . with an impartial insight into the essential nothingness of . . . divine laws" (*Letters,* p. 215)? Are not his marginalia on Martineau, then, at least suspect since they seem to be the product of deep unbalanced depression? Critically, can one rely on them, even in a subordinate way?

In reply, one might first notice two things that Royce did not say in the excerpt just quoted. He did not say that the only time he read Martineau was when he was "in the deepest of my nothingness," nor does Royce make any mention of drafting marginalia in these times. Rather, his initial dullness very likely prevented his writing numerous notes then. Marginalia usually require revived spirits.

In positive and more significant response to this objection, however, it should be said that the intrinsic quality of Royce's marginalia attests to a very perceptive mind. Ralph Barton Perry was arrested so much by one of these marginal notes that he selected it as singularly representative of Royce's central position. (See below, n. 29 in chap. 3.) Finally, apropos of a subordinate use of his marginalia on Martineau, Royce himself provides some guidance. His South Sea reading of Martineau's *A Study of Religion* so deeply influenced him that, although he had criticized and transcended its viewpoint already in 1888 (*Letters*, p. 216), he revealed what it meant to him twenty-eight years later. For in 1916, when selecting only six references for his "Monotheism" article in Hastings's *Encyclopaedia*, Royce included Martineau's *A Study of Religion*, along with Kant and Hegel. In sum, then, available signs suggest that a largely recuperated Royce, duly impressed by Martineau, drafted the marginalia. Accordingly, if used critically and subordinately, the latter may enter into the present study.

2

1. Royce's first trio of books from his Harvard period were *RAP* (1885), *California from the Conquest in 1846 to the Second Vigilance Committee in San Francisco: A Study of American Character* (1886), and *The Feud of Oakfield Creek: A Novel of California Life* (1887). Each was published by Houghton Mifflin of Boston.

2. Royce to Daniel Coit Gilman, February 9, 1888, Gilman Papers, Johns Hopkins University Archives; see *Letters*, p. 211.

3. Clues emerge from the C. R. Lanman diaries of 1888 under dates of January 11, February 28, June 4, and August 4, Harvard Archives.

4. See Royce to Francis Ellingwood Abbot, February 9, 1888, *Letters*, p. 212; and see Abbot to Royce, February 12, 1888, F. E. Abbot Papers, Harvard Archives. Abbot's other letters of this period reveal a temperament markedly different from Royce's.

5. Martineau inscribed opposite the title page of vol. 1: "Professor Josiah Royce with the Author's Respects." See Royce's copy of this 1888 edition reserved in Robbins Library, Harvard.

6. See Royce to James, May 21, 1888, and August 10, 1888, *Letters*,

pp. 217 and 219. The kind letters of introduction from Horace E. Scudder aimed to facilitate Royce's meeting with persons in the Sandwich Islands; see *Letters*, p. 214. Royce's change of travel plans rendered them unnecessary.

7. Royce to C. R. Lanman, May 21, 1888, *Letters*, p. 213.

8. Royce to H. E. Scudder, May 21, 1888, *Letters*, p. 214.

9. Royce to James, May 21, 1888, *Letters*, p. 215. The mention of *"Sonnen und Milchstrassen,"* (suns and milky ways), interestingly alludes to the voluntaristic Schopenhauer's conclusion in *The World as Will and Presentation*. Here Royce does not employ Hegelian terms like Logos or Idea, even though he does describe his own way of putting "the mysteries of absolute idealism." Rather than withdrawing from physical reality, as he found most mystics doing, Royce increasingly emphasized during the next twenty-five years how important it is to stand in loyal affirmation of these "suns and milky ways" and to cooperate with them (see *PC*, 2:308).

10. Royce to H. E. Scudder, May 21, 1888, *Letters*, p. 214.

11. See *Letters*, p. 210, for example. Royce is grateful "for a few charming days" with the Dorrs whose hospitality offered Royce and his wife the mountains and water they loved.

12. See *Letters*, pp. 214-17; *vis medicatrix naturae* (nature's healing force) was the name Royce explicitly gave this tendency when six years later he published "The Case of John Bunyan," republished in his *Studies of Good and Evil* (New York: Appleton and Co., 1898), p. 68 (hereafter *SGE*).

13. Royce to C. R. Lanman, May 21, 1888, *Letters*, p. 213; Royce to James, May 21, 1888, *Letters*, p. 216.

14. See *Letters*, pp. 213-14 and 217.

15. Within a year of his return to Harvard, Royce published his "Reflections after a Wandering Life in Australasia," in the May and June numbers of the *Atlantic Monthly* 63 (1889):675-86, and 813-28. A year and a half later he published his "Impressions of Australia," in *Scribners Magazine* 9 (1891):76-87. Royce's account of his hike in the Blue Mountains occurs in "Impressions," pp. 78-83.

16. "Impressions," p. 79.

17. Ibid., p. 83. After using several pages to describe his encounter with nature in this subjectivity-centered style, for a few lines Royce suddenly shifted into the style of a disciplined behaviorist and recorded only his measurable bodily behavior in response to Wentworth scenery: the panting, heart-leap, and visceral reactions entirely stripped of the felt emotions and moods recorded in his more usual style.

18. Ibid.

19. *SMP*, pp. 342-44, 174-76.

20. He had already described our affective favoritism for "what is near and clear" to us, and our absurd prejudice toward unfamiliar faces and places, in "Reflections," p. 676. A few years after his Australian trip, Royce significantly wove into the historical account of his *SMP* (1892) chapters entitled "The Rediscovery of the Inner Life" and "The Romantic School in Philosophy." In *SMP*'s latter and constructive part, he started by reminding readers that romantic surprises fill the empirical sciences, but fill philosophy "far more so" (*SMP*, p. 311). Here he also made explicit his key distinction between the World of Appreciation and the World of Description, between the self's privately felt affective knowledge and its shareable abstract objective knowledge (*SMP*, pp. 391-96).

21. In "Reflections," "Impressions," and *Letters*, pp. 213-19 and 225.

22. For this close-up of Royce's interaction with nature, see *Letters*, p. 217.

23. E.g., ibid., or *TCWJ*, 1:801-2.

24. LLM, lecture of May 27, 1916, p. 462.

25. *SMP*, pp. 391-96.

26. James to Royce, August 24, 1888, *TCWJ*, 1:802; "your *empirisches Bewusstsein*" is "your consciousness as touched by experience" (rather than as affected by reflection and reasoning).

27. Royce, "Self-Consciousness, Social Consciousness, and Nature," *SGE*, pp. 199 and 204-5. Royce first published the article in *Philosophical Review* 4 (1895):465-85 and 577-602.

28. Nature becomes inert and manipulable only when we secondarily transfigure it into the World of Description, so that we can dominate and develop it for our ends.

29. Royce made this commitment on February 12, 1879, during his "Meditation before the [Golden] Gate." It is published in *FE*, p. 7.

30. See *Letters*, pp. 213 and 217.

31. *Letters*, p. 214.

32. The mutual discovery of these most agreeable companions echoes in Deakin's "Rough Diary, 1888," which first indicates them together, "Tues 5 June. Train with Royce to Sydney," then records long talks and drive to Wentworth Falls, and closes "Wed. 13 June. Goodbye Royce." Deakin Papers, National Library of Australia, Canberra; courtesy of Professor John La Nauze.

33. See "Impressions," p. 78.

34. Royce to Deakin, June 21, 1888, *Letters*, p. 218.

35. Sir Saul Samuel, 1820-1900, was prominent in political life in New South Wales from the 1850s, serving as the Agent General of this colony at London from 1880 to 1897. His 1888 meeting with Royce seems to have occurred during Samuel's return to London after a visit to New South Wales.

36. *PC*, 2:45-48. Besides the Maoris' willingness to take risks to preserve their tribal life and history, the voluntarism of the Australian pioneers battling the desert caught Royce's attention; see "Reflections," pp. 677 and 680.

37. More than two decades after his 1888 voyage, Royce revealed his continuing interest in Australasian primitives, especially in the Maoris of New Zealand. See his 1913 *PC*, 2:45-49, 69, and his article, "Primitive Ways of Thinking, with Special Reference to Negation and Classification," *Open Court* 27 (1913): 577-98. (For Royce's references to his own readings in South Sea culture and history, see esp. pp. 587-88, 592-95, and 597.)

38. Royce to Deakin, June 21, 1888, *Letters*, p. 218.

39. Royce to James, August 10, 1888, *Letters*, p. 219, the source of the present paragraph.

3

1. Royce to C. R. Lanman, May 21, *Letters*, p. 213.

2. Some minor clues exist, such as the one Royce dropped on August 10, 1888, when he wrote James, "I have many things to tell you about philosophy." Thus Royce's May 21 eagerness to share his "new specimen" with James seems to have continued. If so, his insight was developing into "many things." Fittingly enough, since one expects a philosophical insight, if genuine, to deepen and develop.

3. See box E, autograph notebook no. 3, 1884 and 1888, Royce Papers, Harvard Archives.

4. Royce never published this work as sketched in 1888. After his four-page note on "Individuals," drafted on the following day (April 6), Royce made no entry in this philosophical journal until October 31, 1888, when back at Cambridge. So the only extant record of his development during the next forty-four days of his voyage (from April 6 to May 21 when he wrote off Melbourne) seems to be Royce's marginalia on *A Study of Religion*.

5. See box E, autograph notebook no. 3, under dates of October 3 and December 25, 1888, and July 3 and 14, 1889, Royce Papers. All thes

recast outlines reflect Royce's *Religious Aspect of Philosophy* and foreshadow part 2 of his *Spirit of Modern Philosophy.*

6. Ibid., "The World as Paradox and as Ideal," pp. 11-12 (Royce's emphasis).

7. On May 21, 1888, Royce twice told James he read Martineau while aboard and made it clear that by that date he had completed reading, if not all, at least half of Martineau (*Letters*, pp. 215-16). Accordingly, what date is to be assigned to Royce's marginal jottings in *A Study of Religion?* Several signs govern my reply. Ordinarily marginalia are made during one's reading of the volume thus annotated. Further, at no other time in his life have I found Royce expressing an in-depth personal response to Martineau's *A Study of Religion.* But here on May 21, 1888, he readily observes to James that "dear good Martineau runs the same old treadmill for half his book." Thirdly, in the Clarendon Press advertisements at the close of Royce's own second volume of Martineau's *A Study of Religion,* Royce inserted navigational jottings. Thus, for example, not only on p. 37 did he subtract "53.18" from "57.32" to get "4.14" of progress on his voyage, but on p. 39 of these advertisements, his jottings reveal Royce trying to read semaphore signals between his ship and passing vessels. He noted that the signals were this time coming not from "*We,*" but from a sending ship, thus: "*He* (2) R S Q = Thanks Poonah [India], May 6." This dates at least some of Royce's writings in his second volume of Martineau. Moreover, a month earlier, when Royce sketched a sixteen-page outline of "The World as Paradox and as Ideal" under the heading "Barque Freeman, April 5, '88" (see n. 3 above), he never once mentioned Martineau even though he referred to Kant, Spencer, Wundt, and Spinoza in his sketch. This omission would be odd and unlike Royce if by that date he had already encountered the latter three-fourths of Martineau's work with his mind alert enough to pencil critical notations in the margins. (Royce's confession of reading Martineau "in the deepest of my nothingness" may well refer to an attempt during March to leaf languidly through that first quarter of the work which he left practically unannotated.) Finally, the penmanship of Royce's marginalia on Martineau closely parallels that of his May 21 letter to James. It is not as smooth and flowing as his usual healthy hand, such as is found in his August 10, 1888, letter to James. Rather, the style is just a bit abrupt and stiff—neither shaky with sickness nor fully smooth and easy. Hence, the evidence suggests that the date of Royce's marginalia on Martineau's *A Study of Religion* not only coincides with the 1888 voyage but very probably is about early May 1888.

8. *Letters,* pp. 215-16.

9. In his metaphysics lecture of January 11, 1916, Royce pointed to January 11-12, 1883, as the birthday of the religious insight that seeded *RAP;* see LLM, p. 135.

10. See *WI,* 1: xv-xvi, and Clendenning's note 114 in *Letters,* p. 215.

11. Royce had had his "trouble with Continuity" for at least eight years. In 1880 at Berkeley, he felt Shadworth Hodgson's discussion of succession was "full of difficulties and not satisfactory." Then focusing on how we cut past and future from the present, he judged, "The question is who shall now weave up the rope again?" Significantly for his 1892 distinction between "appreciation" and "description," even in 1880 he found that his present act of thinking could not be described, but only experienced. For him, the act of thinking which declares some content present has as its purpose to give significance to, or express the significance of, the present moment. But the thinking act cannot do this unless it constructively postulates an ideal past and future so that in this way an object as present becomes meaningful. In his June 7, 1880, letter to William James, Royce's word and his very long, careful account of his reflection reveals how much, even then, his heart was involved in the "old trouble with Continuity" (*Letters,* pp. 79-83).

12. I here parallel the more general hermeneutic position of John Clendenning (*Letters,* p. 216, n. 115).

13. Martineau, *A Study of Religion,* 1:215-30 (hereafter *SR*).

14. Royce on Martineau, *SR,* vol. 2, opposite title page.

15. Martineau, *SR,* 1:16; see also 1:1.

16. See Royce on Martineau, *SR,* 2:157; notice, too, how this shift from *RAP* is expressed four years later in *SMP,* pp. 408-12 and 457-61.

17. Royce on Martineau, *SR,* 2:30. Royce wanted this distinction maintained. See, e.g., *SGE,* p. xiv.

18. Royce on Martineau, *SR,* 2:136; also opposite title page of vol. 2.

19. See Martineau, *SR,* 1:215-30, where he admitted encountering *RAP* too late to treat it adequately in his overall plan. Yet in his study of theism, he borrowed Royce's phrase, "The World as a Heap of Powers," as the title of his fifteen-page treatment of *RAP.*

20. Ibid.; quotation from 1:215 (punctuation emended).

21. See Royce on Martineau, *SR,* 2:157.

22. Ibid., 1:67, 1:73.

23. Karl Rahner later paralleled Royce's approach by conceiving time and eternity strictly in terms of freedom. For Rahner, "Time is primarily the mode of becoming of finite freedom" (Rahner and Herbert Vorgrimler, *Theological Dictionary* [New York: Herder and Herder, 1965], p.

461). Earlier, Augustine's *Confessions* on time, creation, and salvation had preceded this Roycean approach (see bks. 10-12).

24. Royce on Martineau, *SR*, 1:258.

25. Ibid., p. 340.

26. Royce's 1888 detection and transcription of Martineau's "Alter Ego" theme seems significant because, in his later research and writing on social consciousness, Royce traced the source of this theme to an appreciatively felt contrast effect between *ego* and *alter*. This effect would make possible the recognition of an "other" as also an "ego," yet an Infinite "Alter Ego" as in the present text (see, e.g., *SGE*, pp. 201, 221).

Royce's reading of Martineau's critique of Parker perhaps partly explains why Royce soon asked Horace E. Scudder to reserve Houghton Mifflin's projected volume on Theodore Parker for Royce's then eager and enthusiastic pen (see *Letters*, p. 214). Royce never authored the volume on Parker.

27. See Royce on Martineau, *SR*, 2:9, 28, 50.

28. See, e.g., how it expressed itself four years later in *SMP*, p. 457.

29. See Ralph Barton Perry's "Notes on Individual Authors," under "Royce," R. B. Perry Papers, Harvard Archives. Besides some notes on *WI*, Perry included in this file nothing else on Royce except the present 1888 marginal note, which Perry judged significant enough to copy out longhand.

30. Royce on Martineau, *SR*, 2:194-95. This notation by Royce is metaphysically far more profound, organized, and clear than his April 5 sketch of "The World as Paradox and Ideal" (see n. 3 above).

31. Ibid., 2:157.

32. Ibid.

33. Martineau, *SR*, 1:1.

34. Ibid., 2:229.

35. Royce on Martineau, *SR*, 2:229-30 (Royce's emphases).

36. Milton R. Konvitz, review of *The Basic Writings of Josiah Royce*, ed. John J. McDermott, *Saturday Review*, Jan. 24, 1970, p. 29.

37. Royce on Martineau, 2:238.

38. See *RAP*, pp. 182 and 210, with *FE*, pp. 153 and 191; see *SGE*, pp. 283-84 and 289-90. Compare these with his different "selves" in *CG* (1897), pp. 278-96.

39. Published in the 1897 edition of *CG*.

40. John Dewey later exemplified this position by his a priori "negative wall" erected beforehand against any kind of "supernatural" agent.

41. Royce on Martineau, *SR*, 2:136.

42. Ibid., 2:238-39 (Royce's emphases, but with some punctuation

emended). Although in the middle of this text the word "free," in the phrase "and so not free," is obscure in the original, "free" best fits the extant visible traces and the context.

43. See, e.g., *PC*, 1:271-323.

44. For a fuller Roycean reply, written four years later, see *SMP*, pp. 469-71. Guided by it, I interpretatively fill out in the two following paragraphs the sketch Royce offered in 1888.

God may permit in his limited choosers such hostility and moral deviancy because the True Knower and Supreme Appreciator of moral values is radically and mysteriously present within the "immediate vital issue of every moment" of choice by finite selves. There he most profoundly establishes these moral values and directs the process embodying them. In his practical knowing of the supreme values, he freely appreciates them and, by establishing them, maintains the unity of the moral order amid finite choosers. By willing and embodying these values in the moral universe, he sets them up as the valid norm for all finite knowing, willing, and doing—whether true or false.

The limitations of finite selves—namely, their ultimate moral ignorance and partial unholiness—necessarily make this moral world look dark and chaotic to such selves. But the finite selves' morally responsible interpretation of the Infinite Seer, who is known as present, leads them to discern the fact that hope in such an Alter Ego is fitting. Hence, transcending the limits of their speculative knowledge, they trust in this All-Unifying Knower and All-Holy Self. As Royce had written, "My heart is too little mine to know. I can only hope."

4

1. Royce to James, August 10, 1888, *Letters*, p. 219.

2. See *Letters*, p. 216.

3. See "Impressions," p. 75, and "Reflections," pp. 815 and 818.

4. I am using the phrase "Royce's 1888 grasp of loyalty," or its equivalent, to refer to whatever he thought and expressed on loyalty in 1888 insofar as this is discoverable, mainly from his letters of the time and from his two "Reflections" articles of May and June 1889, as well as from the incidental light cast by his "Impressions" article of 1891. The phrase is a fair enough first approximation since we know that before February 28, 1889, not only had Royce completed these two articles, but also the *Atlantic* had already received, examined, and accepted them, and even informed Royce of a publication date (see *Letters*, p. 228). Quotations in this paragraph are

from Royce to Alfred Deakin, February 28, 1889, *Letters*, pp. 227-30.

5. In 1883-1884, Royce taught Philosophy 4, "Ethics," and in 1885-1886 Philosophy 3, "Elementary Philosophy in Connection with Ethical and Religious Questions" (see *Harvard University Catalogue*, 1882-1888); books he wrote before 1888 are listed in chapter 2, n. 1.

6. *Letters*, p. 216; "Reflections," p. 819.

7. "Reflections," p. 814. The next two paragraphs and their quoted material derive from the same article, pp. 814-16.

8. Years later Royce clarified the point that insight into loyalty allows its possessors to grasp this direction. That is, through the light of loyalty they can see that systems of communities objectively tend to promote the Great Community of all mankind and even to develop the institutional means for realizing such an evolutionary tendency. See Royce's *War and Insurance* (New York: Macmillan, 1914), pp. 24, 68-73, and *HGC*, pp. 64-70.

9. Royce began his account in "Reflections," pp. 676-80, by sketching these common geographical and historical bonds.

10. "Impressions," p. 77

11. "Reflections," p. 820.

12. Ibid., p. 819.

13. "Impressions," p. 86.

14. "Reflections," p. 820.

15. Ibid., pp. 680-81.

16. See Royce's *HGC*, p. 127.

17. "Reflections," p. 822.

18. Ibid., p. 827.

19. See *PL*, pp. 18-20. In the 1888 and 1907 Royce, "cause" was not yet clearly identified with "the interest of the community as such," as it eventually was in his 1915-1916 work.

20. Ibid., p. 816.

21. Ibid., pp. 820, 825, 819.

22. By his final decade, the settling of conflicts of loyalty had become a chief concern for Royce, as *PL*, subsequent lectures on loyalty, and his 1915-1916 extension course in ethics make clear (see Royce Papers, vols. 82-83, 94-95, Harvard Archives).

23. "Reflections," pp. 825, 823, 828.

24. Ibid., pp. 820, 684.

25. Ibid., p. 818.

26. Most popular expositions of Roycean loyalty make no mention of justice—that is, the will to share fairly. Similarly, they often omit Royce's

stress on industrious intelligence at the heart of loyalty. Yet justice and discerning intelligence characterized Royce's 1888 and 1916 conceptions of loyalty, as well as his 1907 popularization of it.

27. "Reflections," p. 818.

28. Ibid.

29. Ibid.; ibid., p. 817; ibid., pp. 817-18.

30. Ibid., p. 828.

31. Ibid., pp. 824-28.

32. Ibid., p. 827.

33. Ibid., p. 824.

34. See *FE*, pp. 6-7.

35. One ingredient the 1889 Royce seems not to have clearly explicated was loyalty's relation to the divine. By 1907, this became *PL*'s philosophy of religion.

36. "Reflections," p. 819; Royce to Deakin, February 28, 1889, *Letters*, p. 229; "Reflections," p. 819.

37. See Royce's more than three long columns describing this self-reliant, loyal backwoodsman in "Reflections," pp. 819-20, the source of the quoted material in the next three paragraphs. That an admittedly verbose Royce penned more than a thousand words to portray to his *Atlantic* readers a man whose character was always "faithful to the value of faithfulness" reflects, among other things, Royce's 1888 interest in loyalty and his deepening penetration of it.

38. Royce's empirical method won this central insight. It arose from his personal reflection on a unique individual and on the constant direction observed in the latter's life course, rather than being seen in a logical deduction from abstract ethical categories.

5

1. "Reflections," p. 681.

2. Ibid., p. 682. Even while recognizing that Royce "got some things wrong" during his brief stay "down under"—for example, perhaps exaggerating the extent of state intervention in Australian life—Professor John La Nauze, historian of Australia and biographer of Alfred Deakin, estimates that during this visit Royce was "an unusually intelligent observer" (La Nauze to John Clendenning, April 28, 1978).

3. Ibid., p. 680.

4. Ibid., p. 679.

5. Ibid., p. 680.

6. Ibid., p. 682.
7. "Reflections," p. 813.
8. Ibid., pp. 813-14.
9. Ibid., p. 815.
10. Measured from his January 1877 lectures on Schopenhauer at Johns Hopkins.
11. "Reflections," p. 681.
12. See *PC*, 2:60-69.
13. "Reflections," p. 681.
14. "Impressions," pp. 83-86.
15. "Reflections," p. 682.
16. Ibid., p. 684.
17. "Impressions," p. 86.
18. Ibid., p. 77.
19. "Reflections," p. 682.
20. Ibid., p. 814. While Royce contrasted the Australian governmental systems with the American on many other lines, he did not highlight one difference. How do the coercions at work in the colonists' less permanent system of parliamentary government compare with the coercions that America's "check-and-balance" system builds among our legislative, executive, and judicial powers?
21. "Impressions," p. 79, from which all quotations in the paragraph are derived.
22. See "Reflections," p. 827.
23. See "Reflections," pp. 682-83 and 686.
24. Ibid., pp. 683-84. In none of my research on Royce have I found that he examined Marxian socialism.
25. Ibid., pp. 682 and 814.
26. Ibid., p. 681.
27. Ibid., p. 682.
28. "Impressions," p. 79.
29. Compare "Reflections," pp. 685 and 816, with "Impressions," p. 85.
30. Compare Royce's novel, *The Feud of Oakfield Creek* (Boston: Houghton Mifflin, 1887), pp. 357-59, with his Australian articles. In the novel, one character, Alonzo Eldon, sets up instruments to propagate Henry George's socialistic ideas. In those pages Royce inserted no such conservative critique as he did later in his Australian articles.
31. "Reflections," p. 820.
32. Ibid.

33. Ibid.

34. Ibid., p. 822.

35. Ibid., p. 823.

36. Ibid., pp. 825-26, from which the quotations in the next two paragraphs are derived.

37. As an instance of such thinking, see Madison Grant, *The Passing of the Great Race* (New York: Braziller, 1916).

38. See Royce's leading essay "Race Questions and Prejudices" in his *Race Questions, Provincialism, and Other American Problems* (New York: Macmillan, 1908), pp. 1-53. On atoning deeds, see *PC*, 1:318-23, 361-64.

39. Royce's perspicacity lay in recognizing how deeply race cuts. From repeated experiences in urban America, one can grant Royce that when two races are mixed without any care for their differences in background, culture, and value systems, or are even forced to live together, the psychological and social health of the individuals and groups involved is often diminished. Thus, provided one basic condition is fulfilled, the usual clustering of the different races into their own groups and that type of resultant racial segregation may promote more psychosocial health. The basic condition is that everyone insists on not tolerating the violation of anyone's fundamental rights—such as are indicated in the United Nations Declaration of Human Rights.

40. "Reflections," p. 826.

41. "Impressions," p. 75.

42. See, for example, *PC*, 2:431; or *War and Insurance*, p. 93; or *HGC*, pp. 54-55.

43. See *PC*, 2:57-105 and Oppenheim, "A Roycean Road to Community," *International Philosophical Quarterly* 10 (September 1970):341-77.

44. "Reflections," p. 825.

45. Ibid.

46. See *PC*, 1: 332-42.

47. Here I am indebted to Drew Christiansen, S. J., et al., "Moral Claims, Human Rights, and Population Policies," *Theological Studies* 35 (March 1974): 83-113.

48. James to G. Croom Robertson, October 7, 1888, *TCWJ*, 2: 43.

49. James to George Herbert Palmer, February 1, 1901, *TCWJ*, 1: 438.

6

1. In *SMP*, we focus particularly on pp. 368-80, guided by Royce's own reference to these pages in his letter to Thomas Davidson of March 21,

1892 (see *Letters*, p. 289)—a reference he repeated in *SGE*, p. 140. Royce selected these pages as a summary of his metaphysical idealism. Only it, he held, successfully solves the epistemological problem of transcending the subjective in knowledge (see *SMP*, p. xiv). "The Implications of Self-Consciousness" appeared in *New World* 1 (1892): 289-310; it was reprinted in *SGE*, pp. 140-68, with slight changes. Royce selected this as one of three restatements between 1885 and 1898 of his "most essential argument"; (see *WI*, I: xv). The unpublished entries (37 pp.) of his philosophical journal under dates of October 31 and December 25, 1888, and July 3 and 14, 1889 also confirm the continuity of his metaphysical speculation. See the beginning of chap. 3 above and box E, autograph notebook no. 3, Royce Papers, Harvard Archives.

2. See *WI*, 1:553-54, n. 1. I base my tentative dating of "around 1891" for this "insight through Schroeder" on an assemblage of four clues. Since Royce reported (ibid.) that this insight first came to him on reading Schroeder's first volume, it could not have occurred before 1890, the publication date of *Algebra der Logik*, vol. 1. Secondly, Royce had a habit of voraciously reading new scholarly books, especially of this kind. Then, too, his 1899 way of referring to this insight suggests it hardly occurred in years recently passed, for in 1899 Royce wrote, "I was *years ago* much struck by the remarkable proof, in the first volume of Schroeder's *Algebra der Logik*" (ibid; emphasis added). Most significantly, however, the endless process of self-reflection is already recognizably present in Royce's 1892 writings (see *SMP*, p. 379, and *SGE*, pp. 145-46).

3. *WI*, 1:553-54, n. 1. From these pages the next two quotations are derived.

4. Ibid., 1:xv, source of the remaining quotations in this paragraph.

5. Royce to James, May 21, 1888, *Letters*, p. 216.

6. *SMP*, pp. 368-80 (see *Letters*, p. 289, and *SGE*, p. 140).

7. *SGE*, pp. ix and 140; see *Letters*, p. 216.

8. *SGE*, p. 146.

9. See Clendenning's n. 115 in *Letters*, p. 216.

10. *SGE*, p. 153.

11. Ibid., p. 141.

12. Cf. *SGE*, pp. 142-43, and *SMP*, pp. 368-70 and 374 with our discussion above, pp. 31-34.

13. *Letters*, p. 216.

14. *SGE*, p. 168. Royce here touches a classic theme akin to Augustine's argument for eternity in his *Confessions*, bk. 11, and perhaps akin to Peter Berger's discovery of the eternal in play which transcends time (see chap. 3

of his *Rumor of Angels*, [New York: Irvington, 1969]). I owe the notice of this parallel to David J. Hassel, S. J.

7

1. See Records of the Bureau of Customs, Record Group 36, National Archives, Washington, D.C., as per letter of Mark G. Eckhoff of the National Archives and Records Service to the author, September 27, 1967. It is as yet undetermined whether Royce first learned in New Zealand that his father had died on June 22 or discovered this only upon his arrival in California.

2. See *Los Gatos News,* August 23, 1888, "A Distinguished Visitor," copy reserved in box 1, folder 3, U.C.L.A. Josiah Royce Memorial Collection. See also the "Tribute to Josiah Royce [senior]," in *Los Gatos News,* August 24, 1888.

3. Royce to James, August 10, 1888, *Letters,* p. 219.

4. Royce to Gilman, September 6, 1888, *Letters,* p. 225.

Index

CPSIA information can be obtained at www.ICGtesting.com
Printed in the USA
BVOW05s2039130416

444129BV00001B/12/P